# TIDY-ISH

## THE ADHD GUIDE TO A MANAGEABLE HOME

## ALEX RIVERS

# CONTENTS

# INTRODUCTION

You know that feeling when you walk into your home at the end of a long day, and instead of relief, you're greeted by overwhelming clutter? Yeah, I've been there too. As a woman with ADHD and a young baby, I've had moments where I've looked around my living room and thought, "How did it get this bad?" One particular day, I couldn't even find a clear spot to change my baby's diaper. That was my breaking point; I knew something had to change.

Hi! I'm Alex, and the struggle you're having is one I know only too well. Living with ADHD can make keeping a tidy home feel like an uphill battle. Trust me, I've been in the trenches, fighting against the constant influx of toys, laundry, and clutter that seems to multiply overnight. But here's the good news: I've discovered that with the right strategies and a healthy dose of humor, it is possible to create a manageable home that works with your ADHD brain, not against it.

This book isn't about achieving picture-perfect, magazine-worthy spaces (let's be honest, who has time for that?). Instead, we're going to find practical solutions that make your life easier and your home more functional. I've poured my heart and soul into creating a guide that's equal parts empathy, real-life success stories, and actionable steps—let's face it, the last thing you need is another book filled with abstract theories and unrealistic expectations.

Throughout these pages, you'll find a mix of personal anecdotes (like the time I accidentally donated my keys to Goodwill), practical worksheets, and tried-and-true strategies from fellow ADHD warriors who have found their way to a more manageable home. We'll dive into the unique challenges of having ADHD: difficulty with task initiation, organization, and maintaining routines. More importantly, we'll focus on flexible, adaptable, and doable solutions for our neurodivergent brains.

Whether you're drowning in a sea of paperwork, struggling to keep up with the dishes, or constantly misplacing your keys (been there, done that!), this book is your lifeline. It's a judgment-free zone where we celebrate progress over perfection and recognize that everyone's journey looks a little different. My goal is to help you understand your ADHD tendencies, develop practical cleaning systems that work for you, and cultivate the motivation to maintain a tidy-ish home.

So, if you're ready to say goodbye to the overwhelm and hello to a more peaceful living space, you've come to the right place. Together, we'll navigate the ups and downs of cleaning with ADHD, armed with a toolkit of strategies, a supportive community, and a generous sprinkle of laughter. Because let's be honest, if we can't laugh at ourselves while fishing our car keys out of the refrigerator, what's the point?

Get ready to embrace the "tidy-ish" life, my friend. It's time to take control of your space, one manageable step at a time. And remember, you've got this! With some guidance and determination, you'll be well on your way to creating a home that feels less like a never-ending chore and more like the sanctuary you deserve.

**Let's do this!**

# PART ONE
# FOUNDATIONS FOR CHANGE

# 1

# LAYING THE FOUNDATION FOR CHANGE

*"Great things are not done by impulse, but by a series of small things brought together."*

— VINCENT VAN GOGH

Not too long ago, I found myself standing in the middle of my living room, surrounded by a chaotic sea of toys, laundry, and an alarming number of coffee mugs. My baby was playing with a sock he found under the couch, blissfully unaware of the cluttered disaster around him. Meanwhile, I stood there, paralyzed, wondering how I'd let things get so out of hand. At that moment, I felt like a captain on a sinking ship—except I wasn't drowning in water, but a never-ending tide of *stuff*.

If you've ever felt overwhelmed by the mess in your home, trust me, you're in good company. That's why we're starting with the groundwork to turn chaos into calm, one step at a time.

# UNDERSTANDING YOUR ADHD BRAIN

Let's begin with your big, beautiful brain. ADHD isn't just about being forgetful or hyperactive; it's a cognitive rollercoaster that affects how we approach everything, from organizing our spices to remembering where we left our keys.

Executive dysfunction is one of the main culprits that gets in our way. That pesky little glitch makes planning, prioritizing, and completing tasks feel like climbing Mount Everest in flip-flops. You might find that you start cleaning the kitchen only to wind up scrubbing the bathtub, hey, it seemed important at the time. Your executive function (or lack thereof) is steering you in unexpected directions.

Hyperfocus, on the other hand, is the superhero of ADHD. It's like having laser vision for tasks that captivate you, whether organizing your bookshelf by color or tackling that daunting junk drawer. Executive Function and Hyperfocus can often work against each other- executive function can make you hyper focus on the exact opposite of what you need to be doing. When harnessed correctly, hyperfocus can be your secret weapon against clutter.

Now, let's talk about strengths and challenges. With ADHD, creativity is often off the charts. This means you're great at thinking outside the box, which can make problem-solving a breeze. Need to find a way to store your ever-growing collection of mismatched Tupperware lids? No problem! You'll invent a system that's not only functional but also uniquely yours, even if nobody else understands it.

But with great creativity comes the not-so-great tendency for distraction. You might start with the best intentions to clean the bathroom, only to find yourself sucked into creating a Pinterest board for bathroom decor for hours. It's a blessing and a curse, this brain of ours, but acknowledging both sides is the first step to managing them.

And then there are those sneaky emotions that creep in when we least expect them. Overwhelm and anxiety are frequent visitors, especially in response to a mountain of laundry or a sink full of dishes. It's easy to feel like you're failing at something as "simple" as keeping a tidy home, but that fear of failure is just your mind playing tricks on you. It's important to remember that these feelings are normal and don't define your worth or ability to manage your space.

This brings us to the ultimate key to unlocking it all: self-awareness.

Understanding your ADHD traits will transform the way you approach cleaning and organization. By recognizing what works for you and what doesn't, you can tailor strategies to your strengths. Self-reflection exercises, like journaling or taking a few moments to assess your feelings before starting a task, can provide valuable insights. It's a personal roadmap for your brain, guiding you to strategies that make sense for your unique wiring.

So, as we dive into this world of tidying with ADHD, remember that knowing yourself is winning half the battle.


## OVERCOMING PROCRASTINATION: STRATEGIES TO START CLEANING

Ah, procrastination, the frenemy we all know too well. It sneaks up on you, like that mysterious sock that keeps reappearing in random places. You promise yourself, "I'll get to it later," but before you know it, later becomes never.

Let's break this down. Procrastination often stems from feeling overwhelmed. You see a mountain of chores, and instead of tackling it, you hide under a metaphorical blanket of Netflix and snacks. If it's not feeling overwhelmed, then it's decision fatigue. By the time you're done deciding what to have for breakfast, lunch, and dinner, your brain is too fried to determine where to start cleaning. The sheer number of choices paralyze you into inaction, leaving you with a mess that only grows larger by the day.

So, how do we kick procrastination to the curb? Enter the "5-Minute Rule." It's simple: commit to cleaning for just five minutes. Set a timer, and when it goes off, you can either stop or keep going. More often than not, that little push is enough to get you rolling. It's like tricking your brain into thinking, "Hey, this isn't so bad after all."

Pair this with the "brain dump" technique: scribble down every task, i.e. pick up trash, hoover, dust shelves and wipe the coffee table cluttering up your mental space. Once it's all out on paper, you can sort through it and decide what to tackle first. It's a way to declutter your brain before your home; with your mind clear, your surroundings don't seem so overwhelming.

Accountability can also be a game-changer. If you're anything like me, you need someone to give you that gentle nudge—or, let's be honest, a firm shove! Find a cleaning buddy, like a friend who also struggles with clutter, and agree to check in with each other. Share your goals for the day and report back once you've made progress. It's incredible how much knowing someone else is counting on you can light a fire under your couch-potato self. You might even turn cleaning into a social event, where you both tackle a room while chatting on the phone, making it feel less like a chore and more like catching up with a friend. Equally, having someone to visit can put a deadline on tidying before they get there!

And let's not forget the wonders of technology! We live in an age where everything can be automated, so why not use it to our advantage? Set reminders on your smartphone to ping you when it's time to tidy up. You might also want to try cleaning apps designed to help you organize tasks and track your progress. These digital tools can act like a little voice in your pocket, gently (or sometimes not-so-gently) reminding you to get off the couch and into action, 'gamify' the process of cleaning, making the process more entertaining. By using technology as your ally, you can transform cleaning from a dreaded obligation into something a little more doable. So, roll up those sleeves, grab your phone, and let's get things done, one small step at a time.

## CREATING A SAFE SPACE: SENSORY-FRIENDLY CLEANING ENVIRONMENTS

Imagine you're on the verge of tackling that cluttered closet when your phone rings, someone starts mowing the lawn next door, and your child decides it's the perfect time to practice their drum solo. Welcome to the sensory overload Olympics, with you the unwilling participant.

For many of us with ADHD, sensory sensitivities play a huge role in how we interact with our environment, making cleaning a daunting task. The roar of a vacuum cleaner might be akin to standing next to a jet engine, and certain cleaning supplies could feel like they're made of sandpaper against your skin. It's not just about noise and texture, either; it's the culmination of these sensory inputs that can make the simple act of tidying up feel like climbing a mountain without any gear.

So, what's a sensory-sensitive soul to do? First, let's tackle the noise. Noise-canceling headphones are a gift from the heavens. Slip them on, and the world becomes a little softer, a little friendlier. Pair them with a playlist of your favorite tunes, and suddenly scrubbing the bathtub seems a bit more bearable. If lighting is your kryptonite, consider soft lighting options. You don't need a full-blown lighting overhaul. Even a simple switch to a lower-wattage bulb or adding a tiny lamp instead of bright overhead lights can turn a harsh space into a cozy nook, making cleaning feel less like a chore and more like a moment of zen.

Now, let's talk about your sensory-friendly cleaning kit. Say goodbye to the overpowering scent of bleach and hello to fragrance-free cleaning products. These gems are not only kinder to your nose but also to your skin, reducing the risk of irritation. You're not just cleaning; you're creating an environment that respects your senses. Stock your kit with microfiber cloths—gentle on surfaces and your hands—and consider using natural cleaning agents like vinegar or baking soda, which are both practical and easy on the senses.

Mindfulness is another tool in our arsenal. It might sound a bit new-age, but hear me out. By focusing on the tactile sensation of cleaning—how the warm water feels on your hands or the smooth glide of a cloth on a countertop—you can turn a mundane task into a meditative experience. This isn't just about being present; it's about finding small joys in the process, allowing your mind to settle into a rhythm that feels natural and unforced. It's the difference between hurriedly rushing through a task and taking a moment to appreciate the simplicity of the action.

## SENSORY-FRIENDLY CLEANING CHECKLIST

- Headphones: For blocking out unwanted noise.
- Soft Lighting: Use lamps or lower-wattage bulbs for a calming atmosphere.
- Fragrance-Free Products: Reduce sensory overload with unscented cleaning agents.
- Microfiber Cloths: Gentle and practical, perfect for sensitive skin.
- Natural Cleaners: Vinegar and baking soda are your best friends.

Creating a sensory-friendly environment isn't just about making cleaning more bearable; it's about crafting a space that feels welcoming and manageable. It's about acknowledging that your sensory experiences are valid and that you deserve a space that caters to your unique needs. By incorporating these strategies, cleaning can be transformed from a dreaded task into a practice of self-care and mindfulness. It's a step towards reclaiming your space and making it truly yours.

## BREAKING FREE FROM PERFECTIONISM PARALYSIS

Picture this: you're standing in your kitchen, surrounded by dishes that have somehow multiplied like gremlins in the night. You think, "I can't start cleaning until I have enough time to make it spotless."

Sound familiar?

That, my friend, is the all-or-nothing mindset at work. Perfectionism is a sneaky little thief, robbing you of productivity because anything less than perfect feels like failure. That voice in your head whispers, "If you can't do it right, don't do it at all." The problem is that this mindset often leads to paralysis, leaving you stuck in a cycle of avoidance and frustration. You wait for the perfect moment to start, but that moment almost never comes. The result? A kitchen that constantly looks like a tornado swept through, and a lingering sense of guilt that follows you around like a shadow.

Let's flip the script. What if you embraced imperfection? What if you let go of the unrealistic expectation that everything has to be done perfectly? The benefits of this mindset shift are enormous. By focusing on progress rather than perfection, you allow yourself to celebrate small victories. Did you wash a few dishes and wipe down the counter? Great! That's progress. Setting realistic expectations means acknowledging that life is messy, and that's okay. Your home doesn't have to look like it belongs in a magazine to be functional and welcoming. By giving yourself permission to do things "good enough," you free yourself from the shackles of perfectionism and open the door to a more manageable, less stressful way of living.

If gradual progress sounds appealing, you'll love the "good enough" principle. It's based on taking incremental steps and making minor improvements without even thinking about perfection. Instead of overhauling your entire house in one weekend (a Herculean task that usually ends in burnout), focus on one room or even one corner at a time. Set incremental goals that are achievable and satisfying. Maybe today you'll tackle the pile of laundry in the bedroom and tomorrow, the stack of papers on the desk. These bite-sized goals are not only easier to manage, but they also provide a sense of accomplishment that fuels further progress. It's like chipping away at a mountain with a small hammer—you'll get there eventually, and the view from the top will be worth it.

## REAL-LIFE EXAMPLE OF BREAKING FREE FROM PERFECTIONISM PARALYSIS

- Testimonial: A reader once shared her story of battling perfectionism. For years, she was trapped in an all-or-nothing cycle, waiting for the rare day when she had the energy to clean her entire apartment—until she decided to try something different. Inspired by the "good enough" principle, she set a timer for 20 minutes and focused solely on tidying her living room. The result wasn't perfect, but it was a vast improvement. Over time, she applied this method to other areas of her home. Now, she maintains a space that's clean enough to be comfortable without the stress of reaching an unattainable standard.

In the end, breaking free from perfectionism is about accepting that life is wonderfully imperfect. It's about realizing that a "good enough" home is a happy home, one where you can relax without the weight of unrealistic expectations hanging over you. So, the next time you find yourself paralyzed by the thought of cleaning, remember that small steps lead to significant changes. Embrace the mess, celebrate your progress no matter how small, and know that you're not alone on this winding path to a tidier, more joyful life.

## EMBRACING FLEXIBILITY: ADAPTABLE CLEANING ROUTINES

Picture this: you've finally psyched yourself up to tackle the looming mess in your house. You're armed with a to-do list longer than a CVS receipt, ready to go at it with the ferocity of a caffeine-fueled squirrel. Then, bam! Life happens. Suddenly, your energy levels dip faster than a rollercoaster, and the rigid routine you so painstakingly planned feels more like a straitjacket than a helpful guide.

For those of us navigating the ADHD landscape, the need for flexibility in our routines isn't just a preference—it's a necessity. Sticking to a strict schedule often sets us up for frustration, especially when our energy levels are as unpredictable as a cat in a room full of rocking chairs. Some days, you're a cleaning dynamo; other days, even getting out of bed is a Herculean task. That's why embracing adaptability isn't just helpful; it's our secret weapon against the clutter.

So, how do we cultivate this magical flexibility? Start with modular cleaning tasks. Imagine your cleaning routine as a series of tiny, independent Lego blocks. Instead of trying to build the entire Death Star in one go, focus on constructing one section at a time. Maybe today, you tackle just the kitchen countertops, and tomorrow, you move on to the living room floor. This modular approach allows you to adjust your tasks based on how you're feeling. If you're having a high-energy day, stack those blocks up and knock out a few tasks. On a low-energy day, give yourself permission to just do one. It's cleaning à la carte, and you're the chef.

Rotating task lists are another gem in the flexible routine toolkit. Think of it like a playlist you shuffle based on your mood. You don't want to be stuck listening to the same song on repeat, and you certainly don't want to clean the same thing every day. By rotating tasks, you keep your cleaning routine fresh and less monotonous. One day, focus on dusting, the next on vacuuming. By keeping it varied, you avoid the dreaded cleaning fatigue that makes even the thought of tidying up feel like pulling teeth.

And hey, don't be afraid to experiment. Maybe you find that cleaning in the morning when the coffee's still kicking works better for you, or perhaps an evening tidy-up session fits best around your work schedule. Try different times and see what clicks. The beauty of this approach is that there's no one-size-fits-all solution. It's about finding what jives with your lifestyle and rhythm.

Now, let me introduce you to the concept of "Flex Days." Think of them as your safety net, those magical days where you can catch up on tasks that fell through the cracks or adjust your routine if things don't go as planned. Maybe you got caught up binge-watching your favorite show (no judgment here) and missed a cleaning session. No worries! Flex Days are there to help you recalibrate and keep things from spiraling out of control. Consider setting aside a specific day each week as your Flex Day. Use it to review your task list, make adjustments, and give yourself a break from the rigidity of a set schedule. It's a weekly reset, a chance to stop and breathe, and maybe even pat yourself on the back for the progress you've made.

In the end, remember that flexibility is giving yourself the freedom to adapt. It's about acknowledging that life doesn't always go according to plan and being okay with that. By allowing for adaptability in your cleaning routine, you're not just managing your home; you're managing your life. So, cut yourself some slack, try new things, and above all, keep it flexible.

## EMPATHY IN ACTION: UNDERSTANDING YOUR UNIQUE EXPERIENCE

Imagine you're having one of those days where even brushing your teeth feels like an Olympic event. You glance around your cluttered living room, feeling like a failure because you can't summon the energy to tackle the chaos. Here's the thing: you're not alone, and you're not failing. Sometimes, we need a little self-compassion to get through these moments. It's about recognizing that some days, our brains just have other plans, and that's okay. Practicing positive self-talk can work wonders. Instead of berating yourself for what's left undone, try acknowledging what you have accomplished, even if it's something as small as getting out of bed. It's your voice—talk to yourself the way you would talk to a close friend.

Recognizing that every ADHD experience is unique is crucial. What works for one person might not work for another, and that's perfectly fine. Tailoring solutions to fit your lifestyle and quirks is the secret sauce. Maybe you thrive on chaos, or you might need a meticulously organized space to function. Whatever your preference, own it! Customize your strategies to fit your needs. Are you a night owl who gets a burst of energy at midnight? Perfect! Schedule your cleaning then. Do you find that cleaning during your favorite podcast makes the time fly by? Go for it! The goal is to create a system that works for you, not against you.

Let me share a story that might resonate. A friend of mine, also living with ADHD, used to feel overwhelmed by the endless lists of things to do. She often compared herself to others who seemed to have it all together. Then one day, she decided to stop following what everyone else was doing and started crafting her own path. She realized she could write her own rules. She began by setting small, personalized goals and celebrated each one. Instead of trying to clean the entire house at once, she focused on one area at a time and gave herself the freedom to leave things unfinished if needed. This shift in mindset transformed her relationship with her space. The key takeaway? It's not about fitting into someone else's mold; it's about finding your own rhythm and dancing to it.

Connecting with a community can be a game-changer. There's nothing quite like knowing others are facing similar challenges. Joining online forums or groups can provide a wealth of support and shared knowledge, and access to resources and tips and tricks you might not have thought of. It's a safe space where you can vent about the mountain of laundry that never seems to shrink or celebrate the small victories like finally getting the dishes done. Within these communities, you'll find empathy, humor, and advice that's grounded in real-life experiences. It's a reminder that you're not isolated in this struggle, and together, we can swap stories, solutions, and maybe even a few laughs.

## ONLINE COMMUNITY SUGGESTIONS

- ADHD Support Forums: A place to connect with others, share your experiences, and find camaraderie in shared struggles.
- Social Media Groups: Platforms like Facebook host numerous groups specifically for ADHD discussions, offering peer support and advice.

By embracing self-compassion, acknowledging individual differences, and connecting with empathetic communities, you can navigate the challenges of ADHD with a bit more ease and a lot more understanding. After all, this is your unique experience, and you deserve a space that feels like home, with all its imperfections.

## BUILDING MOTIVATION: REWARD SYSTEMS THAT WORK

Let's chat about motivation—or, more accurately, the mysterious vanishing act it performs when faced with cleaning tasks. For those of us with ADHD, motivation isn't just a simple "want-to" or "don't-want-to" situation. It's a dopamine-driven roller coaster that often leaves us dangling mid-air, wondering how to get back to the ground. Dopamine, the chemical messenger responsible for pleasure and motivation, doesn't always flow as freely in our brains, making mundane tasks like cleaning feel less like a rewarding activity and more like a torturous chore. You might find yourself eagerly planning a cleaning spree, only to end up binge-watching cat videos instead. It's not laziness; it's a genuine struggle with motivation that's wired into our neurobiology. Understanding this can help us develop strategies that effectively kickstart our motivation engine.

Enter the magical world of rewards, our secret weapon for coaxing motivation out of hiding. Let's be honest: we all love a good reward. It's like dangling a carrot in front of a horse, except instead of a carrot, it's something you actually want (because who wants to clean for a carrot?). Setting up effective reward systems can transform cleaning from a dreaded task into a game with tangible benefits. Start with immediate rewards. Think of them as little pats on the back for completing a task. Cleaned the kitchen? Great! Treat yourself to a square of dark chocolate or a few minutes of your favorite podcast. These instant rewards tap into our dopamine needs, providing that quick hit of satisfaction that keeps us going.

But let's not forget the power of long-term incentives. These slightly larger carrots require a bit more effort, but offer a sweeter payoff. Perhaps you set a goal to keep your living room tidy for a week, and if you succeed, you indulge in a cozy night with a new book or a guilt-free Netflix binge. The key is to choose incentives that genuinely excite you, not just what you think *should* excite you. After all, it's your reward system, so make it work for you!

Let's get creative with our reward ideas, shall we? Small treats don't have to break the bank. It might be a fancy coffee from that café you love or a new playlist to groove to while you clean. Relaxation activities can be a golden ticket for those who prefer something less tangible. Think bubble baths, meditation sessions, or even just a nap (because sometimes, that's the best treat of all). The goal is to keep motivation high by constantly refreshing and surprising yourself with reward options.

Now, let's sprinkle in a bit of science. The concept of positive reinforcement is our friend here. At its core, positive reinforcement involves providing a reward in response to a desired behavior, which increases the likelihood of that behavior being repeated. It's like training a dog, except in this case, the dog is your brain, and the reward is anything that makes it wag its metaphorical tail. By consistently pairing cleaning tasks with rewards, you're essentially rewiring your brain to associate cleaning with positive outcomes. Over time, this can shift your mindset, turning cleaning from a dreaded chore into a satisfying activity.

In the end, remember that motivation is a tricky beast, especially when it comes to cleaning. But with a bit of creativity and the right reward system for you, you can lure it out of hiding. By understanding your dopamine-driven needs and setting up personalized rewards, you're more likely to find cleaning a bit more bearable, if not downright enjoyable. So go ahead, treat yourself, and watch as motivation becomes a more frequent visitor in your cleaning routine.

## THE POWER OF REAL-LIFE SUCCESS STORIES

In a world where cleaning can feel like a never-ending battle against the forces of chaos, there's nothing quite as reassuring as hearing stories from people who've been in the trenches and emerged victorious—or at least with a semi-tidy living room! Take the tale of one reader Natalie, who, after years of living in what she affectionately called "organized mess," decided enough was enough. Armed with little more than determination and a lot of caffeine, she tackled her home one room at a time, documenting her progress. Her secret weapon? Breaking down tasks into bite-sized pieces and celebrating each small victory, no matter how insignificant it seemed. Today, she laughs about how her once-cluttered kitchen is now a space where she can find the spatula when needed, 'Seriously it feels amazing!'

Then there's the case of a young professional James, like many of us, found himself drowning in a sea of paperwork and forgotten gym socks. He discovered that creating a visual checklist was the key to maintaining order. With each item he crossed off, he felt a surge of accomplishment that motivated him to keep going. By the time he reached the bottom of his list, he was amazed at how much more manageable his home felt. His approach involved setting a timer for 20 minutes each day, focusing solely on one area, and refusing to let distractions derail him. These stories remind us that the path to a tidier home is paved with perseverance and creativity.

But what do these success stories really mean for the rest of us? They aren't just feel-good tales; they're blueprints for action. Each narrative offers a step-by-step method for transforming chaos into calm. Start by identifying your most cluttered zone and set a small, achievable goal. Maybe today, you'll clear off the dining table or sort through that mail pile. By breaking down tasks into manageable chunks, you can replicate the success of others and adapt these strategies to fit your life. Use these stories as inspiration, but remember to tailor them to your unique situation. What works for one person might need a tweak or two—or even six!—to work for you.

As you read through these stories, take a moment to reflect on your own experiences. What resonates with you? What strategies have you tried, and how did they work? Use these reflections as a springboard for change. Self-assessment questions can guide you in under-standing your habits and tendencies. Ask yourself, what's holding me back? What small step can I take today to make a difference in my home? By considering these questions, you open the door to mean-ingful progress.

The learning doesn't stop there. Keep exploring, keep experimenting, and keep growing. Dive into books, articles, and resources that offer fresh perspectives and ideas. Join a community of like-minded indi-viduals who can offer support and share their insights. These connections, whether online or in person at local meet ups, can provide knowledge and encouragement. Together, we can learn from each other's triumphs and setbacks, building a network of support that keeps us motivated and inspired.

As you close this chapter, remember that you are not alone in this journey. Real-life success stories are more than just anecdotes; they're proof that change is possible. With determination, creativity, and the right strategies, you can transform your home into a space that reflects your values and supports your well-being. Keep these stories close to your heart, and let them guide you toward a brighter, tidier future.

Here's to the big and small victories and the collective wisdom that propels us forward!

# PART TWO
# MASTERING TIME AND TASK MANAGEMENT

# 2

# MASTERING TIME AND TASK MANAGEMENT

*"I have come to believe that caring for myself is not self-indulgent. Caring for myself is an act of survival."*

— AUDRE LORDE

Imagine you're holding a magic wand that can transform your chaotic days into a series of structured, manageable tasks. Time-blocking is kind of like that wand—minus the actual magic, of course. Instead of waving it around, you'll be waving goodbye to the dreaded time warp that often comes with ADHD. You know, the one where you start checking emails and suddenly it's two hours later, and you're knee-deep in a YouTube rabbit hole about how to train cats to do your bidding. With time-blocking, you can put some order into the chaos, focusing your day into neat little boxes of productivity.

Time-blocking is like Tetris for your schedule. You divide your day into segments, assigning specific tasks to each block of time. This helps you see what needs to get done and when you're going to do it. By structuring your day into these segments, you create a roadmap that guides you through the hours, helping you steer clear of those pesky distractions that seem to pop up from nowhere. For those with ADHD, this structure can enhance focus, reduce overwhelm, and improve overall time management. Think of it as turning your day into a well-conducted orchestra instead of a chaotic jazz jam session.

Setting up these time blocks isn't as daunting as it sounds. Start by identifying the essential tasks you need to tackle, then assign each one a realistic amount of time. Use digital calendars like Google Calendar or apps like Day Optimizer to lay out your blocks. Treat these time slots like appointments you can't miss. You wouldn't skip a doctor's appointment, so don't skip your scheduled time to clean the bathroom either. And be realistic—don't cram too much into one block. Remember, Rome wasn't built in a day, and neither is a spotless house.

Now, let's talk energy levels. We all have them; they just tend to fluctuate more wildly when you have ADHD. Tailoring your time blocks to align with your natural energy peaks and troughs can make all the difference. Are you more of a morning person when the sun is shining and the coffee is hot? Then schedule more demanding tasks like cleaning the kitchen or tackling the laundry mountain for that time. If you're a night owl who thrives in the moonlit hours, save those tasks for later in the day when your brain is firing on all cylinders. The key is to work with your energy, not against it.

Buffer times, my friend, are like the unsung heroes of time management. These little pockets of extra time between tasks act as a cushion for when life inevitably throws a wrench into your perfectly planned schedule. They're the transition periods that allow you to move from one task to another without feeling rushed. Maybe you need a few minutes to mentally switch gears from cleaning the bathroom to organizing the pantry. Or perhaps you just want to sit down with a cup of tea and a good book for a moment. By building buffer times into your schedule, you give yourself the flexibility to breathe and adapt, making your day feel less like a sprint and more like a leisurely stroll.

## TIME-BLOCKING SETUP EXERCISE

1. Identify Tasks: List your daily cleaning tasks.
2. Assign Time Blocks: Use a digital calendar to schedule each task.
3. Align with Energy Levels: Match tasks to times when you feel most energetic.
4. Include Buffer Times: Add transition periods between tasks.

Time-blocking is no magical cure-all, but it's a powerful tool that can help you regain control of your time and tasks. Creating a structured schedule that accounts for your unique energy levels and includes essential buffer times allows you to transform your cleaning routine from a chaotic mess into a series of intentional, manageable actions.

## THE POMODORO TECHNIQUE: CLEANING IN SHORT SPRINTS

Imagine turning cleaning into a series of short, energetic sprints rather than a never-ending marathon. That's the Pomodoro Technique in a nutshell. Named after the tomato-shaped kitchen timer its creator used, this method is all about breaking work into manageable, focused sessions. You set your timer for 25 minutes and dive into a task with laser-like focus, followed by a blissful five-minute break. It's a simple yet effective strategy that works wonders for those of us with ADHD because it plays to our need for both structure and variety. Instead of spending hours getting lost in a task, you tackle it head-on in short bursts, which helps keep fatigue at bay and attention levels high.

Now, let's tailor this technique to suit our cleaning adventures. The traditional Pomodoro might be 25 minutes, but who says we can't tweak it? Some tasks, like sorting through a mountain of laundry, might benefit from a shorter 15-minute block, while a deep bathroom scrub-down might warrant a whole 30. The beauty of this method lies in its flexibility. You can adjust the intervals based on the task at hand and your current energy level. After all, there's no one-size-fits-all when it comes to cleaning—especially with ADHD. Find the sweet spot that keeps you engaged without burning out, and remember, it's all about maintaining momentum without slipping into monotony.

Short sprints come with a slew of benefits. For one, they help reduce the mental fatigue that can accompany long cleaning sessions. Knowing there's a break on the horizon makes the task less daunting. These breaks aren't just for resting, either—they're essential for recharging. Stretch, grab a snack, or bust out a quick dance move to your favorite tune. When you return to your task, you'll find that short breaks can invigorate your focus. Additionally, the Pomodoro Technique can increase task completion rates. When you commit to a task for a set period, you're more likely to see it through, which can be incredibly satisfying.

Let's put this into practice with some real-world scenarios. Picture yourself tackling a kitchen decluttering session. That cluttered countertop—home to yesterday's mail and a rogue banana peel—gets your undivided attention for 25 minutes. You sort, toss, and maybe even discover a long-lost spatula in that time. The timer rings, and it's break time. Five minutes to breathe, sip some water, and perhaps marvel at your newfound counter space. Then it's back at it, maybe shifting your focus to organizing the pantry or clearing out the fridge. Each Pomodoro session propels you forward, turning a daunting task into a series of achievable goals.

Or consider a bathroom cleaning blitz. Set your timer and unleash your inner cleaning beast on the shower tiles, sink, and mirror. The ticking clock adds a sense of urgency, making even grout-scrubbing feel like an epic quest. When the timer dings, reward yourself with a quick scroll through social media or a moment to just chill. As you alternate between cleaning and breaks, this rhythm not only boosts your productivity but also makes the whole process more enjoyable. By the end of your cleaning session, you'll have a sparkling bathroom and a brain that's still firing on all cylinders.

Incorporating the Pomodoro Technique into your cleaning routine doesn't just help you get the job done; it transforms how you approach tasks. It's a method that respects your brain's need for variety and focus, turning cleaning from a chore into a series of manageable, satisfying sprints. So grab that timer, embrace the power of short bursts, and watch your to-do list shrink with each satisfying ding.

## CHUNKING TASKS: AVOIDING OVERWHELM WITH BITE-SIZED STEPS

Ever look at a messy room and feel like you're staring at Mount Everest? You're not alone. Tackling a mountain of clutter can feel like an insurmountable task, especially when your brain is already doing cartwheels trying to focus. This is where task chunking becomes a lifesaver. Think of it as breaking down that mountain into a series of manageable hills. By focusing on one section or item at a time, you can reduce the overwhelming feeling that comes with trying to conquer everything in one go. It's like taking a daunting marathon and turning it into a series of short, achievable sprints. Instead of cleaning the entire living room, you start with the coffee table, then move onto the couch, and so on. This approach makes cleaning more approachable and gives you a series of small wins to keep you motivated.

Creating a checklist is a great way to chunk tasks and keep track of your progress. There's something incredibly satisfying about crossing items off a list, even if it's as simple as "Clear dining table" or "Sort laundry." It turns cleaning into a series of mini-missions rather than an endless chore. Visual aids can also be handy, especially for those of us who are more visually inclined. Try using sticky notes to mark areas you've completed, or take before-and-after photos to see just how far you've come. These tools can provide a tangible sense of progress, transforming cleaning from a dreaded task into a visual journey of accomplishment.

The psychological benefits of task chunking are profound. Each small task you complete provides a sense of accomplishment, a little dopamine hit that says, "Hey, you did it!" This sense of progress is incredibly motivating, especially on days when getting started feels like the hardest part. Completing small tasks can also build momentum, propelling you forward with a newfound sense of purpose. Instead of being paralyzed by the enormity of the task, you find yourself more energized and ready to tackle the next chunk. It's like a snowball effect: small successes lead to bigger ones, and you've made significant progress before you know it.

In practice, task chunking can be incredibly effective. Take the "one drawer at a time" approach, for instance. Instead of attempting to organize an entire dresser in one fell swoop, focus on a single drawer. Empty it, sort through its contents,and only keep what you truly need or love. Once that drawer is done, move on to the next one whenever you're ready. This method applies to any room or area in your home. In the kitchen, you might choose to clean one shelf of the fridge today and tackle the freezer tomorrow. In the bathroom, organize one cabinet and leave the rest for another day. Focusing on one small area at a time makes the task less intimidating and more manageable.

Remember, keeping tasks small and specific is key to effective task chunking. The more detailed your chunking, the easier it is to get started and keep going. Break down tasks into the smallest possible components, and don't be afraid to celebrate each small win along the way. In a world where ADHD often turns everyday tasks into Herculean efforts, chunking provides a practical, empowering way to take control of your environment. It's a strategy that transforms cleaning from a source of stress into a series of satisfying accomplishments.

## TASK STACKING: MULTIPLYING PRODUCTIVITY WITH DUAL TASKS

Task stacking is like the Swiss Army knife of productivity hacks, especially for us folks living with ADHD. The idea is simple: combine two tasks to make the most of your time, turning mundane chores into opportunities for multitasking with a purpose. Imagine it as a dance where each step flows into the next, creating a rhythm that keeps you engaged without tripping over your own feet. It's about finding harmony in chaos, blending tasks that complement each other, and making the most of those precious minutes.

So, let's talk about finding those magical task pairs. Think of it like pairing wine with cheese; instead, you're matching tasks that naturally go hand in hand. Listening to audiobooks while dusting is a classic example. You get to immerse yourself in a good story while your duster does its thing. Suddenly, dusting becomes less of a chore and more of a literary escape. Or consider pairing vacuuming with a podcast. The hum of the vacuum provides a white noise backdrop while the podcast keeps your brain entertained. You might even find yourself looking forward to these cleaning sessions, eager to hear the next chapter or episode.

For those of us with ADHD, finding task combinations that maintain engagement without causing distraction is key. You want tasks that keep your hands busy but leave your mind free to wander, like folding laundry while watching your favorite show. The repetitive action of folding pairs perfectly with the visual and auditory stimulation of TV, keeping you anchored without feeling overwhelmed.

Or, if you're cooking dinner, why not tidy up the kitchen as you go? Chop veggies, then wipe down the counter. Stir the pot, then load the dishwasher. Before you know it, you've cooked a meal and cleaned the kitchen in one go.

But here's the catch—task stacking isn't about piling on as many tasks as possible. It's a delicate balance, and overloading yourself can lead to cognitive overload, leaving you more frazzled than productive. Imagine trying to juggle flaming swords while balancing on a tightrope. Not fun, right? The key is to start small and build up as you get more comfortable. Choose just two tasks that work well together, and focus on completing them efficiently. The goal is to enhance productivity, not create chaos.

It's also important to be mindful of your limits. If you find yourself getting distracted or overwhelmed, it might be time to reassess your task pairs. Not every combination will work for everyone, and that's okay. Be willing to experiment and adapt. Maybe you find that listening to music while cleaning the bathroom works better for you than an audiobook. Or perhaps you prefer to focus on one thing at a time, and that's perfectly fine too. Task stacking is about finding what works for you and creating a system that fits your lifestyle and rhythm.

Task stacking offers a fresh perspective on productivity, turning everyday chores into opportunities for engagement and efficiency. By carefully choosing task pairs that complement each other, you can transform mundane activities into moments of accomplishment and satisfaction. It's a strategy that leverages your strengths while respecting your limits, helping you navigate the challenges of ADHD with creativity and confidence. So grab your duster, queue up that audiobook, and let task stacking work its magic on your to-do list.

# NAVIGATING EXECUTIVE DYSFUNCTION: SIMPLIFIED SYSTEMS

Living with ADHD often feels like you're trying to juggle flaming torches while riding a unicycle. It's a wild act, and executive dysfunction is the pesky clown that keeps trying to trip you up. This little gremlin makes planning and prioritizing tasks feel like solving a Rubik's Cube blindfolded. You know what needs to be done, but getting from knowing to doing? That's a whole different circus. Executive dysfunction takes the straightforward task of cleaning and turns it into an epic quest where the dragon you're slaying is your own inability to decide what to tackle first. You might find yourself staring at a pile of dishes, knowing they need washing, but somehow getting lost in a rabbit hole of reorganizing the spice rack instead. It's not that you don't want to clean; it's that your brain plays tricks on you, making it difficult to start, focus, and complete tasks in any logical order.

Enter simplified systems, your trusty sidekick in this battle against chaos. When your brain is fighting against you, having pre-made task lists can be your secret weapon. Think of these lists as your very own treasure maps, leading you through the maze of cleaning with clear, actionable steps. Instead of standing in the middle of the mess wondering where to begin, you can follow the list and tick off tasks like "wash dishes," "sweep floor," or "take out trash." The beauty of these lists is that they take the guesswork out of cleaning, allowing you to focus less on decision-making and more on execution. Visual organizers play a similar role, clearly outlining what needs to be done and when. For instance, a dry-erase board in the kitchen can serve as a visual reminder of weekly chores, turning abstract tasks into concrete goals. Color-coded charts can also be a game-changer, offering a quick and easy way to categorize and prioritize tasks without overloading your brain.

Building simple, repeatable routines is another strategy to outsmart executive dysfunction. These routines act like a familiar rhythm, guiding you through your day with less mental effort. A daily 10-minute tidy-up session, for example, can work wonders. Set a timer, focus on tidying up one area, and stop when the alarm goes off. This routine reduces the cognitive load of deciding when and what to clean and transforms tidying into a manageable, regular habit. Incorporating these short, predictable bursts of cleaning into your day creates a sense of order and control, which can alleviate the feeling of being overwhelmed by a never-ending list of chores.

Real-life adaptations of these systems show just how effective they can be. One friend of mine, tired of feeling like she was running on a hamster wheel of mess, decided to implement a color-coded cleaning chart. Each day had its own color, and each color represented a specific room and task. Mondays were blue for the bathroom, Tuesdays green for the kitchen, and so on. This visual system helped her break the cleaning process into digestible chunks, making it easier to focus on one task at a time without getting sidetracked. Not only did her home become more organized, but she also found that her stress levels decreased as her environment became less chaotic.

Another example comes from a coworker who swears by her pre-made task lists. Every Sunday, she takes a few minutes to jot down the week's cleaning goals on a notepad. This practice sets her up for success and frees her mind from the clutter of trying to remember everything. By simplifying her systems and routines, she's able to stay on top of cleaning without feeling like she's constantly playing catch-up. These adaptations show that you can navigate executive dysfunction with the right tools and create a cleaner, more organized space that works for you, not against you.

# ROUTINE RESET: REFRESHING CLEANING HABITS

Picture this: you've been following the same cleaning routine for weeks, maybe even months. At first, it was a breeze, like a new pair of shoes that fit just right. But now, it feels more like those shoes have been worn down, losing their charm and comfort. That's where the magic of a routine reset comes in. It's the secret sauce to keeping your cleaning habits fresh and effective. Over time, even the best routines can become stale, like a forgotten loaf of bread at the back of the pantry. They lose their spark, and what once motivated you now just feels like a chore. By periodically hitting the reset button, you breathe new life into your habits, reinvigorating your motivation and making cleaning feel less like drudgery and more like an opportunity for change.

So, when is it time for a routine refresh? It's all about recognizing the signs of stagnation. If you find yourself dragging your feet more than usual, or if your once-efficient cleaning sessions are now taking twice as long, it might be time to shake things up. You may be avoiding tasks altogether, or you may find that your once-satisfying routine no longer leaves you with that sense of accomplishment. These are all red flags that your routine might need a little TLC. It's like your routine is waving a tiny white flag, begging for a makeover to keep it from slipping into the abyss of monotony.

When it comes to revitalizing those cleaning habits, there's a whole toolkit of strategies at your fingertips. Start by introducing new tools into the mix. Sometimes, all it takes is a shiny new gadget or a different cleaning product to reignite your interest. Maybe a new vacuum cleaner that promises to suck up pet hair like a pro, or a fancy mop that makes you feel like a cleaning wizard. Rotating the order of tasks can also work wonders. If you've been starting with the bathroom, why not switch it up and tackle the living room first? This simple change can make the process feel fresh, keeping your brain engaged and curious about what comes next.

Flexibility is your best friend when it comes to routines, and adapting them based on changing needs and preferences is key. Think of your cleaning routine as a living, breathing thing that evolves with you. Your energy levels have shifted, or the seasons have changed, bringing new challenges like muddy boots and pollen-covered surfaces. Adjust your routine accordingly, embracing the ebb and flow of life rather than fighting against it. Instead of rigidly sticking to a fixed schedule, allow yourself the freedom to adjust tasks and timing as needed. This adaptability keeps things interesting and ensures that your routine remains effective and aligned with your current lifestyle.

In my own experience, seasonal adjustments can be a game-changer. As the weather changes, so do the demands on your home. Spring might mean more time spent dusting and airing out rooms, while winter calls for cozying up and focusing on indoor maintenance. By aligning your cleaning tasks with the seasons, you keep things fresh and address your space's unique needs throughout the year. This proactive approach helps prevent your routine from growing stale, ensuring that you're always one step ahead of the game. Embrace the beauty of routine resets, and watch as your cleaning habits transform from a mundane task into a dynamic, engaging practice.

## OVERCOMING TIME BLINDNESS: TOOLS TO STAY ON TRACK

Ever find yourself knee-deep in a cleaning task, only to surface hours later in a daze, unsure if it's still Tuesday or if you've somehow skipped to next week? Welcome to the world of time blindness, a common experience for many with ADHD. It's like having a clock that runs on whims rather than ticks, making it easy to lose track of time while engrossed in a task—or even while avoiding one. You start off with the best intentions to clean the bathroom, and suddenly it's dinner time, and you've only managed to clean the sink. Time seems to melt away, slipping through your fingers like sand, leaving you wondering where the day went. But fear not, because there are ways to keep track of time and bring it back under your control.

One of the most straightforward tools to combat time blindness is the humble timer. A kitchen timer, a smartphone alarm, or even a fancy digital watch can serve as your personal timekeeper, bringing you back to reality when your mind starts to wander. Set it for a specific duration, like 20 or 30 minutes, and focus on your cleaning task until it goes off. This simple act can anchor you in the present, providing a tangible reminder that time is, indeed, passing. Visual countdowns, like hourglasses or digital timers with visual progress bars, can also be incredibly effective. They give you a visual representation of time slipping away, making it easier to stay engaged and adjust your pace. It's like having a little visual nudge that says, "Hey, keep going—you're almost there!"

Routine time checks are another weapon in your arsenal against time blindness. Imagine them as pit stops during your cleaning race, moments to pause, reflect, and recalibrate. Set periodic reminders on your phone or use a smartwatch to gently prompt you to check in with yourself. Are you still on task? Has your focus drifted to organizing your sock drawer instead of vacuuming the living room? These regular check-ins can help you catch yourself before you go too far off track, allowing you to steer yourself back to the task at hand. They also provide an opportunity to reassess if you need to adjust your time blocks, perhaps adding a few extra minutes to complete a task or wrapping up early if you're ahead of schedule.

Let's look at practical scenarios where these tools and techniques can be applied to your daily cleaning routine. Picture starting your day with a quick scan of your living space, setting a timer to tackle the most pressing mess first. Perhaps it's the kitchen, where dishes have taken over the counter like an invading army. You set your timer for 30 minutes, and in that time, you focus solely on washing and putting away dishes. As the timer ticks down, you might work more efficiently, motivated by the visual countdown. When it rings, take a moment to check in with your progress. If you're on track, celebrate with a short break. If not, adjust your plan and decide on the next task to conquer.

Or consider a weekend cleaning spree. You've decided to tackle multiple rooms, but you know that time has a way of slipping away. Set alarms at regular intervals to remind you to switch tasks, ensuring you don't spend all afternoon lost in the depths of a single closet. Use visual countdowns to keep the momentum going, constantly reminding you that there's a world outside your cleaning bubble. This approach keeps you on track and adds fun, turning cleaning into a series of time-based challenges that keep you engaged and focused.

Time blindness can make cleaning feel like a never-ending saga, but with the right tools and strategies, you can make time your ally rather than your adversary. By incorporating timers, visual count-downs, and routine time checks into your cleaning routine, you can maintain awareness of time and keep those slippery minutes from sneaking away. It's all about finding what works for you, experimenting with different methods, and embracing the journey to a more organized, time-conscious life.

## PRIORITIZATION TECHNIQUES: TACKLING WHAT MATTERS MOST

Imagine staring at a to-do list that seems to scroll endlessly, with each task shouting for attention like a gaggle of hungry seagulls. Prioritization is your secret weapon against this chaos. By figuring out what truly matters, you ensure that the critical tasks are completed, leaving the less urgent ones to squawk another day. It's about transforming that overwhelming list into a series of manage-able steps, each with its own place in line. Prioritization helps you focus your energy where it's needed most, ensuring that the dishes get done before you start alphabetizing your spice rack or ironing your socks.

Now, you might wonder how to decide which tasks deserve your attention first. Enter the Eisenhower Box method, a nifty little trick that helps you categorize tasks by urgency and importance. Picture a square divided into four quadrants. The top left holds urgent and important tasks—like cleaning up a surprise coffee spill before it seeps into your carpet. The top right is for important but not urgent tasks, such as organizing your pantry. Bottom left is for urgent but not important tasks, which might include answering that email about a sale you're not interested in. Finally, the bottom right is where tasks go to wither and die—not urgent nor important, like rearranging your bookshelf by color. This method gives you clarity, helping you see which tasks need immediate action and which can wait.

Another helpful approach is ABC prioritization. Think of it as assigning each task a letter grade based on its priority. A-tasks are top priority and must be done today, like taking out the trash before the collection truck arrives. B-tasks are important but have a bit more wiggle room, like vacuuming the living room before the week-end. C-tasks are those you'd like to get done but won't lose sleep over if they don't happen, like finally dusting that top shelf. This system simplifies your decision-making process, allowing you to tackle tasks systematically without feeling overwhelmed.

Balancing competing tasks can feel like juggling flaming torches while riding a unicycle, but a priority matrix can help. Imagine a grid where you plot tasks based on their priority and deadline. This visual tool helps you see what needs your attention now and what can be pushed to later. It's like having a GPS for your cleaning journey, guiding you through the winding roads of household chores without missing a turn.

Let's explore some real-world examples of how prioritization can be applied to cleaning. Consider a weekly cleaning schedule versus a daily one. On a weekly level, you might prioritize deep cleaning tasks like scrubbing the bathroom and mopping the floors, which are crucial for maintaining a hygienic home. On the other hand, daily tasks might include things like doing the dishes and taking out the trash—those quick jobs that keep chaos at bay. By differentiating between weekly and daily tasks, you ensure that essential chores get done without overwhelming yourself with endless tasks.

As we bring this chapter to a close, remember that prioritization isn't about doing everything at once. It's about focusing on what matters most and letting the rest fall into place. By using methods like the Eisenhower Box, ABC prioritization, and priority matrices, you can tackle your cleaning tasks with confidence and clarity. These techniques offer a roadmap for navigating the maze of household chores, ensuring you spend your time and energy on the things that truly need it. So grab your metaphorical map, chart your course, and step into a world where cleaning is no longer a chaotic scramble but a series of intentional, prioritized actions. And as you move forward, keep in mind that every step—big or small—is progress toward a more organized, manageable home.

# PART THREE
# ADHD-FRIENDLY
# CLEANING SYSTEMS

# 3

# CREATING ADHD-FRIENDLY CLEANING SYSTEMS

---

*"Nothing is impossible. The word itself says 'I'm possible!'"*

— AUDREY HEPBURN

---

I magine walking into a room and feeling a sense of calm wash over you. The space isn't just tidy; it's visually organized to make your brain do a happy little dance. For those of us with ADHD, visual cues are as essential as morning coffee. They help us navigate our spaces without having to dig through piles of whatever-we-saved-for-later. Why? Because our brains love visual order! When everything has its place, it reduces the mental clutter that can lead to feeling overwhelmed. Think of visual organization as the GPS for your home's chaos. Instead of getting lost in the Bermuda Triangle of misplaced socks and forgotten bills, you have clear paths to follow.

So, how do you conquer the clutter and create spaces that speak to your ADHD brain? Let's start with clear storage bins. They're like see-through treasure chests where you can store everything from craft supplies to seasonal sweaters, all while being able to see exactly what's inside. No more playing hide-and-seek with your belongings. Open shelving units are another game-changer. They display your favorite items and serve as gentle reminders of where things belong. It's like having little signposts around your home, guiding you to put things back where they came from. Plus, they make it easier to grab what you need without the hassle of opening and closing doors.

Creating visually appealing spaces is like painting a masterpiece. You don't need to be Picasso, but a few color-coded labels can transform a chaotic mess into a harmonious symphony. Use different colors for different categories—red for kitchen supplies, blue for office materials, and so on. It's not just about aesthetics; it's a practical way to organize your life. Minimalist design principles can also help. Think clean lines, less clutter, and more room to breathe. By reducing visual noise, you create an environment that's both welcoming and functional. It's like giving your brain a much-needed vacation from the chaos.

Don't underestimate the power of visual aids. Picture labels can turn your world into a beautifully organized gallery. Stick a picture of shoes on your shoe bin or a photo of cereal on the pantry shelf. It's a simple yet effective way to ensure everything finds its way back home. Vision boards for your goals can also keep you motivated. Whether you want to declutter your wardrobe or finally tackle that junk drawer, having a visual reminder of your objectives can help you stay on track. It's like having a personal cheerleader, minus the pom-poms.

Regular visual assessments are the secret sauce to maintaining this visual harmony. Think of it as a monthly check-in with your space. Take photos of each room when it's tidy and use them for comparisons later. It's a great way to spot the slow creep of clutter before it becomes a full-blown takeover. Plus, seeing your space in photos can provide a fresh perspective, helping you notice things you might overlook in the day-to-day. It's like having a mini-makeover every month, keeping your spaces as fresh as a daisy.

## VISUAL ORGANIZATION EXERCISE

- **Clear Storage Bins**: Identify areas that need organizing and find transparent bins that fit the space.
- **Open Shelving Units**: Choose a room to install open shelving and select items to display neatly.
- **Color-Coded Labels**: Assign colors to categories and label storage areas accordingly.
- **Picture Labels**: Create or print pictures for common items and attach them to relevant storage spots.
- **Vision Boards**: Design a vision board with your cleaning goals and display it where you'll see it often.
- **Monthly Photo Comparisons**: Take before-and-after photos of each room and compare them monthly to track progress.

Visual organization isn't just about making things look pretty. It's about creating a system that makes sense to you and guides you through the chaos with ease and clarity. You can transform your home from a cluttered mess into a well-oiled machine by focusing on visual cues. So grab those labels, snap some photos, and let's get organized!

## MINDFUL CLEANING: BRINGING PEACE TO THE PROCESS

Picture this: you're knee-deep in laundry, the TV blaring, and your phone buzzes with notifications. It's chaos, and your mind is racing faster than a caffeinated squirrel. Enter mindful cleaning—a little oasis of calm in the whirlwind of chores. Mindfulness is about being present, fully engaging with the task at hand, and letting go of distractions. Imagine taking a deep breath, feeling the gentle swish of water as you wash dishes, and focusing on the sensation of the warm suds. Being present in the moment transforms cleaning from a mundane task into a meditative practice. It's about tuning into your senses, noticing the textures, sounds, and even the smells around you. Instead of rushing through chores, take a moment to set an intention before you begin. Perhaps it's to create a peaceful environment or to simply enjoy the process. A little deep breathing can work wonders, grounding you in the moment and helping you tackle tasks with a newfound sense of calm.

Incorporating mindfulness into your cleaning routine can be a game-changer. Start by focusing on your senses. Notice the feel of a dust cloth gliding over surfaces or the rhythmic swoosh of the vacuum. Engage with the task, allowing your mind to settle into the rhythm of the activity. Setting an intention is another powerful tool. Before you begin, take a moment to decide what you hope to achieve—whether it's a sense of calm, a tidy space, or simply the satisfaction of a job well done. As you clean, keep that intention in mind, letting it guide your actions and focus. This approach not only enhances concentration but also reduces anxiety. By anchoring yourself in the present, you give your mind a break from the usual whirlwind of thoughts.

The benefits of mindful cleaning extend beyond a tidy home. It offers a chance to pause, breathe, and reset. Stress melts away as you immerse yourself in the task, finding satisfaction in each completed chore. The act of cleaning becomes less about the end result and more about the experience itself. Your concentration improves, allowing you to complete tasks more efficiently. Anxiety takes a backseat as you engage fully with the present moment, creating a sense of peace and accomplishment.

Let's explore some real-life examples of how to practice mindful cleaning. Start with mindful dishwashing. Rather than rushing through the pile of plates, slow down and focus on the task. Feel the warmth of the water, notice the bubbles, and appreciate the simple act of making something clean. It's about finding joy in the little things, transforming a routine chore into a soothing ritual. Or try vacuuming with awareness. Listen to the hum of the vacuum, feel the vibrations through your hands, and watch as dust and dirt disappear. It's a chance to zone in, tune out distractions, and relish the momentary escape from the chaos.

Mindful cleaning isn't about achieving perfection. It's about embracing the task as an opportunity to connect with the present, to find peace amid the routine. By bringing mindfulness into your cleaning routine, you create a space that's tidier and more harmonious. It's a gentle reminder that cleaning isn't just a chore—it can be a moment of tranquility, a way to find calm in the everyday. So next time you grab that broom or dustpan, remember to pause, breathe, and be present. Who knew cleaning could be so zen?

## SENSORY TOOLS FOR CLEANING: FROM NOISE CANCELLING TO AROMATHERAPY

Cleaning can feel like a sensory assault when you have ADHD, with every clang and whiff threatening to derail your best intentions. Many of us face aversions to strong scents and an acute sensitivity to loud noises. It's like trying to focus while a rock band practices in your living room. The smell of bleach might send you running for the hills, and the roar of a vacuum cleaner can feel like nails on a chalkboard. But fear not, because there are ways to turn down the volume on these sensory challenges and create a more pleasant cleaning experience.

Start with sensory-friendly cleaning products. Unscented cleaning agents are your best friends here. They do the job without assaulting your nostrils, letting you clean without the overpowering scent of artificial fragrances. Soft cleaning cloths can also make a world of difference. Instead of those scratchy, irritating options that feel like you're scrubbing with sandpaper, opt for microfiber cloths. They're gentle on surfaces and your hands, making cleaning a tactile delight rather than a chore you dread.

Now, let's sprinkle a little magic with aromatherapy and sound tools. An essential oil diffuser can be a game-changer. Imagine filling your home with calming scents like lavender or eucalyptus while you clean. It's like a spa day for your senses. These diffusers gently waft your chosen aroma throughout the room, transforming the act of cleaning into a soothing ritual. Pair this with a white noise machine to mask those jarring sounds that typically disrupt your focus. Whether it's the hum of a gentle breeze or the soft patter of rain, these soundscapes can create a backdrop that keeps your mind engaged without distraction.

Personalization is key when it comes to sensory tools. Not all scents or sounds will resonate with everyone, so it's vital to find what works for you. Experiment with customized scent blends in your diffuser. Maybe you love the invigorating mix of citrus and mint, or perhaps a comforting blend of vanilla and chamomile is more your speed. It's your space, so make it smell like home. Similarly, craft a personal playlist for cleaning sessions. Whether it's classical tunes that help you focus or upbeat pop hits that turn cleaning into a dance party, the choice is yours. Tailor these tools to fit your preferences, creating an environment that feels just right.

SENSORY TOOLS CHECKLIST

- **Unscented Cleaning Agents**: Stock up on fragrance-free products to reduce olfactory overload.
- **Soft Cleaning Cloths**: Invest in microfiber cloths for a gentle, effective clean.
- **Essential Oil Diffuser**: Choose calming scents to enhance the cleaning atmosphere.

- **White Noise Machine**: Select a soundscape that masks disruptive noises and maintains focus.
- **Customized Scent Blends**: Experiment with different essential oils to find your ideal aroma.
- **Personal Playlists**: Create a playlist that motivates and energizes you during cleaning.

With the right sensory tools, you can transform cleaning from a cacophony of chaos into a symphony of serenity. It's all about finding the right balance—muting the distractions while amplifying the elements that bring you joy. So grab those unscented cleaners, plug in your diffuser, and let the calming sounds and scents turn your cleaning routine into a sensory-friendly sanctuary.

## SIMPLIFYING ORGANIZATION: ADHD-FRIENDLY METHODS

Life can feel like a game of Whac-A-Mole when it comes to keeping things organized. As soon as one mole—or pile of clutter—gets whacked, another seems to pop up. For those of us with ADHD, this is a daily reality. That's where the "one-touch rule" comes in. Imagine handling each item only once, putting it where it belongs immediately instead of letting it roam free across every surface. It's like a little game with yourself—can you resist the urge to put that mail down on the counter instead of putting it in its rightful spot? By adopting this rule, you cut down on the dreaded pile-up. Pair this with clear and accessible storage solutions, and suddenly the chaos starts to make sense. No more digging through a drawer's bottomless pit to find that elusive charger. Everything has a home, and it's easy to reach, making tidying up less of a chore and more of a quick pit stop in your day.

Let's talk about sorting techniques that are as simple as pie. A method called "Keep, Toss, Donate" works wonders. Picture yourself standing in front of a cluttered closet. Instead of deciding on each item's fate right then and there, sort them into three piles. Keep the things you love and use, toss the ones that are beyond repair, and donate the clothes that are still in good condition but haven't seen daylight in years. It's like a cleansing ritual for your wardrobe, and who doesn't love a good cleanse? Daily declutter routines can also save your sanity. Set aside just ten minutes a day to tackle one small area. Maybe it's the kitchen counter today and the bathroom sink tomorrow. These bite-sized sessions prevent clutter from spiraling out of control and keep your space feeling fresh.

Keeping things simple and straightforward is the name of the game. Regular reviews and adjustments are part of the package. Think of it as a friendly check-in with your space. Is your organizational system still working for you, or has it turned into more of an obstacle course? Maybe that box labeled "Miscellaneous" has morphed into a black hole. If something isn't working, change it up. Adjust, adapt, and keep things moving. It's not about perfecting it the first time but finding what works for you now. Just like updating your wardrobe for the seasons, your organizational systems need a refresh now and then.

Take the capsule wardrobe, for example. It's all about minimizing your clothing options to a curated selection of pieces that you love and wear often. Not only does it make getting dressed a breeze, but it also keeps your closet organized and clutter-free. It's like having your own personal boutique. In the kitchen, a minimalist setup can work wonders. Imagine opening your cabinet to find only the essentials—no more mismatched Tupperware lids or that one pan that's more rusty than the pan. This simplicity makes cooking and cleaning up a joy rather than a chore.

Organizing doesn't have to be a Herculean task. By implementing ADHD-friendly methods like the one-touch rule, simple sorting techniques, and regular reviews, you can create a space that's easy to maintain and adapt. It's about making your environment work for you, not adding to your stress. So, grab those storage bins, sort through your things, and create a system that brings clarity to the chaos. After all, who said organizing can't be a fun and rewarding adventure?

## CLUTTER BLINDNESS: SEEING CLUTTER ANEW

Ever notice how you can walk past the same pile of clutter every day without really seeing it? That's clutter blindness for you. It's like that old pair of socks you meant to throw out but keep forgetting about. Over time, you become desensitized to the mess, and it just blends into the background, becoming part of the scenery. This phenomenon can wreak havoc on maintaining a tidy home, especially when your brain is already juggling a dozen other things. When clutter becomes invisible, it silently grows until you trip over a stack of magazines one day and wonder how it got there. For those with ADHD, this desensitization can be particularly tricky. Our minds are often racing ahead, leaving little room for noticing the gradual build-up of stuff that transforms a space from cozy to chaotic.

But fear not, there are ways to tackle clutter blindness head-on. One approach is to employ fresh perspective techniques, which are like giving your eyes a pair of glasses for clutter. Try looking at your space from a different angle. Sit on the floor or stand on a chair to get a new viewpoint. Sometimes, a change in perspective is all it takes to spot the clutter that's been hiding in plain sight. Another effective strategy is photographic assessments. Snap a few pictures of your rooms and take a look at them later. You might be surprised at what jumps out at you. Photos have a way of highlighting what your mind has chosen to ignore. When viewed through a camera lens, that forgotten laundry pile suddenly becomes glaringly apparent.

Preventing clutter blindness requires a proactive approach. Consider incorporating regular decluttering practices into your routine to catch clutter before it becomes invisible. Weekly declutter sessions can be a lifesaver. Set aside a specific time each week to tackle one area of your home. It could be the kitchen counters one week and the bathroom cabinets the next. These sessions help prevent clutter from accumulating and make it easier to maintain a tidy space. Regular decluttering can transform a chaotic house into a more manageable home, one small step at a time.

Take a page from those who have successfully managed clutter blindness. One reader shared her story of triumph over the never-ending paper trail in her home office. She used to overlook the stacks of documents as part of the decor until, one day, she decided enough was enough. Armed with a fresh perspective and a determination to declutter, she tackled the piles, sorting through them with a critical eye. Now, she conducts weekly decluttering sessions, ensuring that her workspace remains clutter-free. Another reader found success by using photographic assessments to tackle her cluttered living room. By taking photos and reviewing them, she was able to spot the clutter she had been blind to for months. Armed with this newfound awareness, she was able to make meaningful changes to her space.

Clutter blindness doesn't have to be a permanent condition. You can regain control of your space by employing fresh perspectives, photographic assessments, and regular decluttering practices and banish clutter to the sidelines. It's about making the invisible visible, transforming your home from a cluttered maze into a sanctuary of calm. So grab that camera, shift your angle, and say goodbye to clutter blindness.

## INCORPORATING TECHNOLOGY: APPS AND TOOLS FOR ORDER

In the age of smartphones and smart homes, technology can be your greatest ally in the quest for a tidy space. Picture this: your phone gently pings to remind you it's time to tackle those dishes or sort that laundry, all while you're miles away thinking about your next

Netflix binge. Reminder apps are like having a personal assistant who's not afraid to nudge you when you've veered off course. They can help you break free from the time warp that often accompanies cleaning tasks. You're brought back to reality with a simple alert, ready to conquer the next item on your to-do list. Digital organization tools are equally handy. They allow you to map out cleaning tasks in a way that feels less like a burden and more like a game plan. These tools provide a structured way to approach tasks, ensuring nothing falls through the cracks.

Let's talk about apps that can streamline your cleaning routine. Todoist is a fantastic option for task management. It allows you to create detailed lists, set priorities, and even collaborate with others if you share chores with family or roommates. It's like a digital command center for your cleaning operations. Another app worth checking out is Tody, which focuses on cleaning schedules. It tracks when you last cleaned each area of your home and reminds you when it's time to do it again. Think of it as a cleaning coach, cheering you on from the sidelines, keeping you accountable, and making sure you don't forget to dust those pesky baseboards.

Setting up these tech solutions might feel daunting, but fear not. Start by syncing calendar reminders with your phone or digital calendar. Choose specific times for cleaning tasks and set recurring alerts. This way, you establish a routine without having to rely solely on memory, which can be a bit unreliable when ADHD is in the mix. Voice-activated tasks are another tech-savvy solution. If you have a smart speaker, set it up to remind you of tasks. You can say, "Hey Alexa, remind me to clean the bathroom at 3 PM," and let it do the remembering for you. It's like having a digital butler in the corner of your room, always ready to assist.

Now, let's address the potential for tech overwhelm. We've all been there—downloading every app under the sun only to find ourselves more frazzled than before. The key is to limit app usage. Choose one primary tool that resonates with you and stick with it. Maybe

Todoist is your jam, or perhaps Tody is your go-to. Avoid the temptation to juggle multiple apps, as this can create more chaos than clarity. Keep it simple, and let your chosen tool become your trusty sidekick in the battle against clutter. By integrating technology into your cleaning routine, you create a system that's tailored to your needs, helping you stay organized without feeling overwhelmed.

So, embrace the digital age and let technology lend a hand in your cleaning endeavors. With the right apps and tools at your disposal, you'll be better equipped to tackle each task with confidence and ease, turning cleaning from a dreaded chore into a manageable part of your day.

## FLEXIBLE ORGANIZING: ADAPTING SYSTEMS TO YOUR LIFESTYLE

For many of us with ADHD, life is like trying to juggle flaming torches while riding a unicycle on a tightrope. It's unpredictable, constantly shifting, and occasionally, a bit of a circus act. That's why having flexible organizing systems is not just helpful—it's vital. Our needs and priorities change faster than a toddler's mood swings, and rigid systems can crumble under the weight of life's unpredictability. Imagine trying to fit a square peg into a round hole; it just doesn't work. We need systems that can bend and stretch with us, adapting to the chaos rather than fighting against it.

Creating these adaptable systems is like building with LEGO blocks instead of cement bricks. You want modular storage solutions that you can rearrange as needed. Think of stackable bins that can be shuffled around depending on what you need to store. Today it's art supplies, tomorrow it's winter clothes. The beauty lies in its versatility, allowing you to tweak your storage to fit your ever-changing requirements. Interchangeable task lists are another gem. Imagine a list where you can swap out tasks based on urgency, mood, or even how much caffeine you've had that day. It's about having a system that's as dynamic as you are, one that moves with your energy levels and goals.

Personalization is the secret ingredient to any successful system. It's like adding your favorite toppings to a pizza—sure, cheese and pepperoni are classic, but maybe you're in the mood for pineapple today. Customizable planning tools let you tailor your organizing system to suit your lifestyle. Whether it's a planner you can fill in as you go or a digital tool that lets you adjust your schedule on the fly, the key is making it work for you. Don't be afraid to experiment with different methods. If one approach doesn't fit, try another. There's no one-size-fits-all when it comes to organizing, especially with an ADHD brain.

Let's explore some real-world scenarios where flexible systems shine. Imagine rotating cleaning schedules—one week you tackle the kitchen first, and the next, it's the bathroom. This approach keeps things fresh and prevents burnout by allowing you to focus on different areas at different times. Multi-purpose storage is another lifesaver. Picture a bookshelf that doubles as a room divider or a storage ottoman that holds blankets and toys. These dual-purpose solutions maximize space and efficiency, adapting to whatever life throws your way.

Living with ADHD means embracing the unexpected; your organizing systems should do the same. By focusing on flexibility, personalization, and adaptability, you create an environment that supports your lifestyle rather than constrains it. So embrace the chaos, and build a system that flows with you, not against you.

## EMBRACING IMPERFECTION: LETTING GO OF FLAWLESSNESS

We've all been there: staring at a cluttered room, picturing a pristine, magazine-ready space, and feeling utterly paralyzed. Perfectionism is like that annoying friend who insists on pointing out every tiny flaw, making even the smallest tasks feel monumental. It's easy to fall into the trap where the pursuit of flawlessness becomes a form of procrastination. You think,"If I can't make it perfect, why bother at all?" This mindset turns cleaning into a daunting mountain, one that seems insurmountable with every glance. The dishes pile up, the dust bunnies multiply, and before you know it, you're buried under the weight of your own expectations.

But here's the secret: progress matters more than perfection. Let's say it together for the folks in the back. Embracing the"good enough" principle is like taking a deep breath after holding it for too long. Instead of aiming for a spotless home, celebrate the small wins. Did you clear off the kitchen table today? Awesome! Managed to vacuum the living room? High five! Each little victory is a step forward. These achievements, no matter how minor they seem, deserve recognition. They're the building blocks to a more manageable, less stressful living space.

Shifting your focus from an unattainable ideal to tangible progress reduces stress and fosters a sense of accomplishment and pride.

To help release the grip of perfectionism, start by setting achievable goals. Instead of planning to deep-clean the entire house in one afternoon, break it down. Tackle a single room or even just one corner of a room. This approach makes the task feel less overwhelming and more like a series of manageable steps. It's like eating a giant pizza slice by slice rather than trying to stuff the whole thing in your mouth at once—way more satisfying and less likely to cause a mess! By setting realistic goals, you allow yourself the grace to make progress without the pressure to achieve zen-like perfection in every corner.

Let's talk about those who've embraced imperfection and found peace. Take my friend, who used to obsess over every speck of dust on her shelves. One day, she decided to let go. She set a timer for fifteen minutes each day, focusing on one area with the understanding that it wouldn't be perfect—and that was okay. Over time, her home became more organized, not because she achieved perfection, but because she consistently made progress. Another friend of mine found success in embracing the "good enough" ideology when it came to laundry. Instead of sorting every piece of clothing into precisely folded stacks, she decided that neatly folded was good enough. The result? A more relaxed approach to laundry day and a little extra time for herself.

Embracing imperfection isn't about settling for less; it's about recognizing that life is beautifully messy. By letting go of the need for flawlessness, you free yourself to enjoy the process and appreciate the progress you make. Your home doesn't have to look like a showroom to be welcoming and comfortable. So, give yourself permission to be imperfect. Celebrate your wins, set realistic goals, and remember that a bit of dust never hurts anyone. As we wrap up this chapter, think of imperfection as your ally, not your adversary. It's your permission slip to live a little more freely without the chains of perfection holding you back. Whether you take on the world or just that pile of laundry, remember: good enough is more than enough.

# MAKE A DIFFERENCE WITH YOUR REVIEW
## UNLOCK THE POWER OF ENCOURAGEMENT

*"Small acts, when multiplied by millions of people, can change the world."*

— HOWARD ZINN

Keeping a home tidy when you have ADHD can feel impossible. But small steps, done over time, create real change. And just like tidying, your review can help others take their first step toward a home that feels calm and manageable.

Would you help someone like you—someone who wants a tidy home but doesn't know where to start?

My mission with Tidy-ish is to make tidying feel less overwhelming and more doable for ADHD brains. But to reach more people, I need your help.

Most readers choose books based on reviews. Your words could be the nudge that helps someone stop feeling stuck and start making progress. It takes just a minute, but your review could help...

...one more person let go of cleaning shame.

...one more ADHD brain finds a system that actually works.

...one more home feels like a peaceful place to be.

Your support means the world to me. Thank you for being part of this journey!

Alex Rivers

# 4

# EMOTIONAL AND PSYCHOLOGICAL STRATEGIES FOR SUCCESS

---

"Every time you try, you grow. Every time you grow, you rise."

— UNKNOWN

---

D o you ever find yourself staring at an old pair of jeans, remembering when you wore them to that fantastic concert back in the day? Or maybe you have a mug that belonged to your grandma, and every time you see it, you feel like she's sitting there with you, sipping tea and sharing stories. It's not just stuff; each home item has a little story, a narrative that ties into our emotions and memories. For those of us navigating the ADHD waters, these emotional ties can add layers of complexity to decluttering. It's not just about tossing things out; it's like deciding which memories to keep and which to let go. And let's be honest, deciding to part with that concert t-shirt feels like saying goodbye to a tiny piece of your past.

Emotional attachments can make decluttering feel like an emotional obstacle course. Gifts, for instance, can carry the weight of sentimentality, like that vase from Aunt Betty that's not quite your style but reminds you of her kindness. Heirlooms are another category, often laden with memories of those passed on or moments that shaped our lives. Letting go of these items is akin to letting go of the people or experiences they represent. But here's the thing: a home filled with too much sentimentality can become overwhelming, like trying to read every chapter of your life at once. It's about finding a balance and honoring the past while making room for the present.

One strategy to navigate this emotional labyrinth is creating a memory box. This isn't just any box; it's a curated collection of treasures that genuinely hold meaning for you. Think of it as a tiny museum dedicated to your personal history. You don't need to keep every single birthday card or souvenir spoon; instead, choose a few key pieces that evoke the strongest memories. This way, you can preserve the essence of your experiences without drowning in clutter. Plus, having a designated space for these items means you can revisit them whenever nostalgia hits, like flipping through an old photo album. It's a way to cherish the past without letting it spill into every corner of your home.

Mindful decision-making is crucial in this process. Before you toss or keep an item, pause and ask yourself, "Does this serve me now?" It's a simple question but can help cut through the emotional noise. That old sweater reminds you of a friend, but a photo could capture its essence without taking up space if it's been unworn for years. Mindfulness helps you weigh the value of an item against the practicality of keeping it, allowing you to be present in your decision-making. It's about choosing to live with intention, creating a home that reflects who you are today rather than who you used to be.

## REFLECTION EXERCISE: YOUR SENTIMENTAL SPECTRUM

- **Take a moment** to gather a few items you're attached to.
- **Reflect** on why each one holds meaning. Is it the memory, the person, or the object itself?
- **Decide** which items to keep, donate, or photograph instead.
- **Create** your memory box with the chosen treasures.

Let me share the story of someone who successfully navigated this emotional terrain. A reader once told me about her journey with decluttering the contents of her childhood bedroom. It was like stepping into a time capsule, each item tugging at her heartstrings. She found it difficult to discard anything, fearing she'd lose the memories tied to them. But armed with a memory box and mindful decision-making, she began sorting through the clutter. She kept a few special mementos, like a seashell from a family vacation and a note from a dear friend, letting go of the rest. It wasn't just about clearing space; it was about releasing the weight of the past and creating room for the future.

In the end, decluttering with heart is about finding peace with your possessions, honoring what matters, and gently letting go of what doesn't. It's okay to feel attached; it's part of being human. But creating a home that's more about living than reminiscing is also OK.

## TACKLING NEGATIVE PAST EXPERIENCES: MOVING FORWARD

Cleaning, or even just the thought of it, can sometimes bring up a whole mess of feelings. It could be the memory of a failed cleaning attempt that left you staring at an even bigger mess than when you started. Or perhaps it's the nagging voice in your head reminding you of the countless times you promised to get organized but never quite got there. These past experiences can hang over you like a rain cloud, dampening any motivation to tackle the clutter now. It's not just about the physical act of cleaning, but the emotional baggage that comes with it. You might recall those times when your efforts fell short, leaving you with a sense of defeat that's hard to shake. And let's be honest, who hasn't felt like a cleaning failure at least once? It happens to the best of us. But, those past struggles don't have to define your present or future efforts. Acknowledging these experiences is the first step in releasing their grip and moving forward with a fresh perspective.

Sometimes, letting go of these negative experiences requires emotional spring cleaning. Journaling can be a potent tool in this process. Grab a notebook and jot down your thoughts about past cleaning mishaps. Write about what happened, how it made you feel, and what you might have learned from it. There's something cathartic about putting pen to paper, as if the act of writing can help purge those lingering feelings of failure. And who knows, you might even find a bit of humor in those past disasters when you see them written out. Mindfulness meditation is another way to release emotional weight.Take a few moments to sit quietly and focus on your breath, allowing thoughts to come and go without judgment. This practice can help you detach from the emotions tied to your cleaning past, creating space for new, more positive experiences.

Once you've acknowledged and released the emotional ties of past failures, it's time to look ahead with fresh eyes.Reframing these experiences can be incredibly empowering. Instead of viewing them as failures, consider what lessons they might hold. Did you learn that trying to clean the entire house in one day is a recipe for burnout? Great! That's valuable insight. Use it to shape a more manageable approach moving forward. Shift your focus from what didn't work to what you can do differently now. This perspective fosters a more positive outlook and equips you with the tools to approach cleaning with renewed confidence.

Positive affirmations can also play a crucial role in building confidence and resilience. Think of them as little pep talks for your brain. Create a few affirmations that resonate with you, like "I am capable of creating a tidy space" or "Every small step is progress." Say them out loud each day, especially before diving into cleaning tasks. These affirmations act as mental armor, protecting you from the self-doubt that might try to creep in. Over time, they can help rewire your mindset, replacing negativity with a sense of empowerment and capability.

## AFFIRMATION EXERCISE: BUILDING CONFIDENCE

- **Choose** an affirmation that speaks to you, like "I am making daily progress."
- **Repeat** it daily, especially when negative thoughts arise.
- **Reflect** on how these affirmations make you feel over time.

In the end, addressing negative past experiences is about recognizing their impact and moving forward with a lighter heart. It's about shifting from self-criticism to self-compassion, allowing you to embrace cleaning as a positive, achievable part of your life. Remember, the past is just that—the past. You have the power to create new experiences and redefine what cleaning success looks like for you.

## BUILDING RESILIENCE: OVERCOMING CLEANING SETBACKS

Resilience in cleaning isn't about having a spotless home all the time. It's about bouncing back after the chaos has had its way with your living room. Think of it as taking a deep breath, looking at the mess, and saying, "Challenge accepted," even if your brain is doing somersaults at the thought. Resilience is that inner strength that says, "I can do this," when you're faced with a mountain of laundry or a sink full of dishes that looks like it hasn't seen the light of day in weeks. It's the mental fortitude to tackle these setbacks with a sense of determination and maybe even a bit of humor, because who doesn't need a good laugh when they find socks in the freezer?

One practical way to build resilience in your cleaning habits is to set small, achievable goals. Instead of telling yourself, "I need to clean the entire house today," break it down into bite-sized pieces. Start with the goal of clearing off one surface, like the dining table or the coffee table. Once you've successfully tackled that, celebrate your progress. Treat yourself to a cup of tea or a few minutes of doing absolutely nothing. By acknowledging and celebrating these small wins, you're reinforcing positive behavior, which can make the whole process feel less like an uphill battle and more like a series of manageable steps. It's like leveling up in a video game, where each completed task unlocks the next level of satisfaction.

Let me share a story about a reader who found resilience through her cleaning challenges. She was one of those people who felt defeated every time her home slipped back into chaos. It was like a never-ending cycle, and she often wondered if she'd ever get the hang of it. One day, she decided to try a different approach. Instead of focusing on the entire mess, she set a simple goal: keep the kitchen counter clear for a week. Just one week. As soon as she achieved this, she celebrated by watching her favorite movie, popcorn in hand. That small success gave her the confidence to tackle other areas, one at a time. Now, she views setbacks as opportunities to learn and adapt, rather than reasons to give up.

Adopting a growth mindset can be a game-changer in building resilience. It's about seeing setbacks not as failures but as opportunities for growth and learning. So, the next time you stare at that pile of clutter that seems to multiply overnight, ask yourself, "What can I learn from this?" Perhaps you realize that leaving mail on the counter is a recipe for disaster, or that you need to declutter more often to avoid the avalanche of stuff. Shifting your perspective opens the door to personal growth, turning what might feel like a setback into a stepping stone toward a more organized and manageable home.

## RESILIENCE EXERCISE: SETBACKS AS STEPPING STONES

- **Identify** a recent cleaning setback and reflect on what led to it.
- **Consider** what you can learn from the experience. Is there a pattern? A habit to change?
- **Set** a small, specific goal to address the issue.
- **Celebrate** your progress with a reward, reinforcing positive behavior.

Building resilience in the context of cleaning is about more than just tidying up. It's about cultivating a mindset that embraces challenges and sees the value in each experience. By setting small goals, celebrating progress, and adopting a growth mindset, you can transform cleaning from a dreaded task into a practice that empowers and uplifts you. So take on those setbacks, and bounce back with renewed energy and confidence.

## MOTIVATION TECHNIQUES: SUSTAINING ENERGY AND FOCUS

Living with ADHD often feels like being in a constant tug-of-war with motivation. One minute, you're ready to conquer the world; the next, you're struggling to muster the energy to peel yourself off the couch. This rollercoaster is partly due to fluctuating energy levels that can make maintaining enthusiasm for tasks like cleaning feel like chasing a mirage. You might start the day with grand plans to organize your closet, only to find yourself sidetracked by a sudden need to alphabetize your spice rack instead. It's not laziness; it's just how the ADHD brain operates, constantly seeking novelty and stimulation, leaving mundane tasks like cleaning on the back burner.

Understanding motivation is key to navigating these challenges. Intrinsic motivation refers to doing something because it's personally rewarding, not for some external reward. Think of it as the internal cheerleader that gets you moving because you genuinely enjoy the task. Setting intrinsic goals can be a game-changer. Perhaps you tidy your room because you love the peace it brings, not because someone told you to do it. On the flip side, extrinsic motivation relies on external rewards. It's like dangling a carrot in front of a donkey, except the carrot is that new book you've been eyeing, and the donkey is, well, you. Both types of motivation have their place, and using them strategically can help you maintain momentum even when your energy is doing the cha-cha.

Personalized motivation strategies are like custom-tailored suits; what works for one person might not suit another. Creating a motivational playlist can be a fantastic way to keep your energy up. Fill it with tunes that make you want to dance around the living room, even if you're just vacuuming. Music can lift spirits and make even the dullest tasks feel a bit more exciting. Visualizing a tidy home can also be a powerful motivator. Close your eyes and imagine walking into a clean, organized space. Feel the calm wash over you, the satisfaction of knowing where everything is. This visualization can serve as a mental anchor, reminding you of the reward waiting at the end of your efforts.

Maintaining focus during cleaning tasks can be challenging when your mind is doing cartwheels. One trick is to use focus-enhancing scents. Certain smells, like peppermint or lemon, have been shown to improve concentration and alertness. Consider lighting a scented candle or using an essential oil diffuser while you clean. It's like giving your brain a little nudge to stay on track. Another way to maintain focus is to break tasks into smaller, more manageable chunks. Instead of telling yourself to clean the entire kitchen, focus on one part at a time, like the countertops or the fridge. This makes the task less daunting and provides a sense of accomplishment with each completed step.

One reader shared how she keeps a small bottle of peppermint oil nearby when tackling her cleaning list. Whenever she feels her focus slipping, she takes a quick whiff, and it's like her brain gets a little jolt of clarity. This simple trick has helped her stay on track, even when distractions threaten to pull her away. Another reader swears by her motivational playlist, which she updates regularly to keep it fresh. For her, the music turns cleaning from a chore into a mini dance party, infusing energy, and fun into the routine.

Navigating motivation with ADHD involves understanding the unique hurdles and leveraging both intrinsic and extrinsic motivators to keep you engaged. By personalizing your strategies and finding ways to sustain focus, cleaning can transform from a dreaded task into an achievable, even enjoyable, part of your day.

## FINDING JOY IN CLEANING: MAKING IT ENJOYABLE

Whoever said cleaning had to be a dreary chore clearly never tried turning it into a dance party. The truth is that cleaning can become a joyful activity when you sprinkle in some fun elements. For those of us with ADHD, the idea of scrubbing floors or dusting shelves might initially sound as appealing as watching paint dry. But what if we flip the script and make cleaning something we look forward to? It's about finding those little pockets of joy and injecting them into your routine. Imagine dancing around the living room with a broom as a makeshift microphone, belting out your favorite tunes. Suddenly, those dust bunnies don't stand a chance against your one-person concert.

Music is a game-changer. Create a playlist that gets your toes tapping and your heart pumping. Think of it as the soundtrack to your cleaning adventures. The right song can make wiping down counters feel like an epic montage in a movie where you're the star. And if music isn't your thing, consider turning cleaning into a game. Set a timer and see how many tasks you can complete before it buzzes. Challenge yourself to beat your previous time or reward yourself with a treat once you finish. It's about transforming cleaning from a mundane task into something that feels more like playtime.

Finding joy in cleaning isn't just about making the process more enjoyable—it has tangible benefits too. When you're having fun, motivation naturally increases. It no longer feels like you're dragging yourself through the motions; instead, you're engaged, present, and even excited to tackle the next task. This shift in perspective can also reduce stress. Rather than dreading the pile of dishes waiting in the sink, you see it as an opportunity to unwind and have a little fun. It's like discovering a hidden gem in an otherwise ordinary day, turning the mundane into something memorable.

I remember a reader sharing her experience with finding joy in cleaning. She always felt overwhelmed by the sheer volume of chores, viewing them as an endless cycle with no end in sight. One day, she decided to try something different. Armed with a playlist of her favorite 80s hits, she turned cleaning into a dance-off. The kitchen became her stage, and her mop, a dance partner. She looked forward to these cleaning sessions for the first time, not just for the satisfaction of a tidy home but for the joy it brought her. It became a form of self-care, a way to let loose and recharge.

Another reader found joy by incorporating her love for storytelling into her cleaning routine. She would listen to audiobooks while tidying up, immersing herself in different worlds as she scrubbed and organized. It was like multitasking in the best possible way— her home got cleaner, and she enjoyed a good story. These personal stories highlight the power of finding joy in everyday tasks, proving that with a bit of creativity, cleaning can become a source of happiness rather than a source of dread.

## OVERCOMING OVERWHELM: STRESS REDUCTION TECHNIQUES

Ever walk into a room and feel like you're entering a battlefield of clutter? If you have ADHD, this scenario can feel all too familiar. Overwhelming clutter is like a constant background noise that makes it hard to focus on anything else. It's not just the physical mess; it's the mental clutter that comes with it. The stress of not knowing where to start can paralyze you, turning a simple tidying task into a Herculean effort. The thought of sorting through piles of laundry or stacks of paperwork can trigger a stress response that feels like a weight pressing down on your chest. This stress isn't just inconvenient; it can sap your energy and leave you feeling defeated before you even begin. For many, the clutter becomes a vicious cycle —stress leads to avoidance, which leads to more clutter, and so the cycle continues.

Breaking this cycle starts with stress reduction methods designed to calm the chaos. Deep breathing exercises are a simple yet effective way to soothe the mind. Take a few moments to inhale deeply through your nose, hold for a count of four, and then exhale slowly through your mouth. This practice helps slow down your heart rate and brings your focus back to the present. It's like telling your brain, "Hey, it's okay, we've got this." Progressive muscle relaxation is another technique worth trying. Start by tensing the muscles in your toes, then slowly work your way up the body, releasing tension as you go. It's like giving yourself a mini massage from the inside out, helping to release the physical stress that often accompanies mental clutter.

Simplification and prioritization are your best friends when it comes to reducing cleaning-related stress. Instead of tackling everything at once, focus on one area at a time. Start with a small, manageable space, like a corner of your living room or a single kitchen counter. By breaking down the task, you reduce overwhelm and create a sense of accomplishment as you complete each section. This method makes the task feel more doable and provides a clear starting point, removing the ambiguity that often leads to stress. Prioritizing tasks helps you focus on what truly matters, ensuring that the most pressing needs are addressed first. It's like having a roadmap that guides you through the cluttered maze, one step at a time.

Consider the story of a friend who, overwhelmed by their cluttered home, decided to try these techniques. They started small, focusing on one room—the bedroom. Every morning began with deep breathing exercises, setting a calm tone for the day. Instead of diving into the whole house, they prioritized decluttering a single drawer each day. This gradual approach made the task less daunting and allowed them to see tangible progress without feeling overwhelmed. Week by week, their stress levels decreased as their living space became more organized. The act of focusing on one area at a time, coupled with stress reduction techniques, transformed what once felt like an insurmountable challenge into a series of manageable tasks.

Taking the time to identify sources of stress and applying these methods can help turn cleaning from a stress-inducing task into a more peaceful endeavor. It's about finding balance and creating a space that feels less like a burden and more like a sanctuary. With the proper techniques, you can face the clutter head-on, reducing stress and creating a more harmonious living environment.

## CREATING A SUPPORTIVE ENVIRONMENT: FAMILY AND FRIENDS

Living with ADHD and trying to keep a clean home can sometimes feel like you're in a one-person band, frantically trying to play every instrument at once. But what if you could turn that solo act into a full-blown orchestra, with each family member playing their part? That's the magic of creating a supportive environment. Having a team to back you up can transform cleaning from a lonely struggle into a shared adventure. Imagine a family where everyone pitches in, turning an overwhelming task into a collective effort. It's like having your own cheerleading squad, ready to boost your spirits when motivation dips and to celebrate with you when you achieve tidiness triumphs. Encouragement from family members can be the wind beneath your cleaning wings, lifting you up when the clutter threatens to pull you down. A kind word or a simple gesture of help can make all the difference, transforming cleaning into a team sport where everyone wins.

Building a support network starts with clear communication. It's like crafting a cleaning chart that outlines who does what and when, ensuring everyone knows their role in keeping the home ship's shape. Family meetings can be a great place to kick off this conversation. Gather around the kitchen table, coffee mugs in hand, and discuss the cleaning tasks at hand. It's an opportunity to lay out expectations, share the workload, and maybe even negotiate who gets to tackle the dreaded bathroom. Creating a family cleaning schedule can help keep everyone on the same page, like a roadmap guiding you through the wild terrain of household chores. Assign tasks based on individual strengths and preferences, ensuring each person feels accountable and appreciated. And don't forget to factor in a bit of flexibility—after all, life has a way of throwing curveballs, and the ability to adapt is key to keeping things running smoothly.

Friends can also play a pivotal role in your cleaning support network. Enter the concept of cleaning parties—yes, you heard that right. Invite a few friends over, crank up the music, and tackle your home together. It's like a social gathering with a productive twist. Not only do you get the satisfaction of ticking cleaning tasks off your list, but you also get to enjoy the company of your favorite people. You might even find that cleaning with friends turns into a rhythm where you swap stories, share laughs, and conquer clutter faster than you ever could alone. Plus, the promise of a reward—a pizza party or a movie night—at the end can be an excellent motivator for everyone involved. It's cleaning with a side of camaraderie, proving that many hands really do make light work.

Let me share a story from a reader who found success through family support. She once felt like she was fighting a losing battle against clutter, with her small apartment constantly teetering on the edge of chaos. Frustrated and overwhelmed, she decided to enlist the help of her family. They held a meeting and created a simple cleaning schedule, assigning tasks and setting aside a few hours each weekend for a family cleaning blitz. To her amazement, this collaborative effort lightened the load and brought them closer together. They celebrated their clean home with a fun family outing, reinforcing the idea that working as a team led to shared success and enjoyment.

Creating a supportive environment isn't just about dividing tasks; it's about fostering a sense of unity and shared responsibility. When everyone plays a part, cleaning becomes less of a chore and more of a shared experience. It's about turning the daunting task of maintaining a tidy home into a group effort, where support and encouragement flow freely, making the journey less daunting and much more enjoyable.

## THE ROLE OF SELF-COMPASSION IN CLEANING

Self-compassion is like giving yourself a warm hug when you feel like drowning in a clutter. It's about being gentle with yourself, especially when things don't go as planned, and understanding that everyone has their messy days. In the context of cleaning and organizing, self-compassion means treating yourself with kindness instead of criticism. We often hold ourselves to impossible standards, like expecting our homes to look like the polished pages of a lifestyle magazine. But let's be honest, life isn't always Instagram-worthy. Embracing self-compassion allows you to acknowledge that it's okay if the dishes pile up or if the laundry mountain resembles

Everest. It's about recognizing your efforts and giving yourself permission to be human.

Practicing self-compassion in your cleaning routine can be a game-changer. Start by acknowledging your efforts rather than focusing solely on the outcome. Did you manage to clear off the kitchen counter today? Fantastic! It doesn't matter if the rest of the house is still a bit chaotic. Celebrate the small victories, because they're stepping stones to a more organized space. Taking breaks is another way to weave self-compassion into your routine. Cleaning marathons might sound productive, but they can quickly lead to burnout. If you find yourself getting overwhelmed, give yourself a breather. A short walk, a cup of tea, or even a moment to sit and breathe can recharge your mental batteries, making the task feel less daunting. It's about pacing yourself and understanding that slow and steady often wins the race.

The benefits of self-compassion extend beyond just feeling good in the moment. When you're kind to yourself, motivation tends to flourish. Instead of dreading the next cleaning session, you approach it with a lighter heart, knowing that perfection isn't the goal. This shift in mindset can also reduce anxiety. When you let go of the need for everything to be spotless, guilt and shame lose their power over you. You're no longer weighed down by unrealistic expectations, and you find an increased sense of self-esteem in their place. Your worth isn't tied to the state of your home; it's rooted in who you are. By practicing self-compassion, you cultivate a more positive relationship with both yourself and your environment.

I remember hearing from a reader who embraced self-compassion in her cleaning routine. She used to beat herself up whenever her home wasn't impeccably tidy, feeling like she'd failed some invisible test. But one day, she decided to try a different approach. She started each cleaning session by acknowledging what she'd accomplished the previous day, however small. If she felt overwhelmed, she allowed herself a break without feeling guilty. Over time, she noticed a change—not just in her home but in her outlook. Cleaning became less of a chore and more of a practice of self-care. She discovered that she was more motivated to maintain a tidy space by being kind to herself. Her story is a reminder that self-compassion isn't a detour from productivity; it's a direct path to a more fulfilling experience.

Self-compassion is an essential ingredient in the recipe for a harmonious home. Embracing kindness and understanding creates an environment where motivation and self-esteem can thrive. As we wrap up this chapter, remember that the journey to a tidy home is as much about caring for yourself as it is about managing your space. The next chapter I'll explore practical implementation and sustainability, ensuring that our discussed strategies become lasting habits.

# PART FOUR
# PRACTICAL STRATEGIES FOR SUSTAINABLE TIDINESS

# 5

## PRACTICAL IMPLEMENTATION AND SUSTAINABILITY

---

*"Done is better than perfect."*

— SHERYL SANDBERG

---

Have you ever stood in the middle of your living room, surrounded by a whirlwind of clutter, and thought, "Where do I even start?" It's like staring down a dragon of disorganization, armed with nothing more than a feather duster and a prayer. But here's the secret: even the most epic quests start with a single step. This chapter isn't about slaying dragons in one fell swoop; it's about taming them one scale at a time. Think of it as the art of small beginnings, where you build momentum and confidence by tackling tiny tasks. Focusing on manageable chunks creates a ripple effect that transforms your home from chaos to calm.

Let's dive into the concept of starting small. Imagine choosing just one room—like the kitchen, where those rogue coffee mugs and snack wrappers seem to party all night. Instead of trying to conquer the entire space simultaneously, focus on a single surface. Maybe the countertop has become a magnet for clutter or the dining table doubling as a paperweight collection. By zeroing in on one area, you make the task less daunting. It's like zooming in on a single puzzle piece instead of staring at the whole jigsaw. You might find that once you've tackled that one surface, you're inspired to move on to another. Before you know it, you've created a domino effect of tidiness.

Setting achievable goals is the next step in your journey to a cleaner home. Aiming for perfection is like trying to capture a unicorn—fun to dream about but not practical. Instead, set realistic targets, like dedicating ten minutes daily to cleaning. You'd be amazed at what a difference this can make. A daily 10-minute power clean is like a shot of espresso for your home: quick, invigorating, and surprisingly effective. Set a timer, turn on your favorite tunes, and see how much you can accomplish in a short burst. This approach not only keeps the overwhelm at bay but also builds a habit of regular maintenance, making your home feel more manageable over time.

To help you get started, let's create a basic cleaning schedule. Picture it as your trusty map, guiding you through the wilderness of household chores. List the tasks that need attention, then assign each to a specific day. Monday could be for kitchen counters, Tuesday for the bathroom sink, etc. Keep it simple and flexible, allowing room for life's inevitable curveballs. The goal isn't to create a rigid system but to provide a gentle structure that supports your cleaning efforts. Think of it as a dance routine: you have a framework, but there's plenty of room for improvisation.

## SUCCESS STORY: SMALL STARTS, BIG CHANGES

Meet Sam, a reader who felt overwhelmed by the clutter in his apartment. He decided to start small, focusing first on his desk, which had become a catch-all for everything from bills to half-empty coffee cups. By dedicating just 10 minutes each day to decluttering, he gradually expanded his efforts to other areas. Within a month, Alex transformed his living space into a sanctuary of calm and order. What began as a series of small steps grew into a sustainable routine, proving that even the tiniest beginnings can lead to significant progress.

Starting small isn't just a strategy; it's a mindset. It's about giving yourself permission to begin where you are, with what you have, and trusting that each small effort contributes to a more significant transformation. By focusing on one room, one surface, and one goal at a time, you're not just cleaning your home—you're reclaiming it. So grab that feather duster, put on your favorite playlist, and celebrate each small victory. You're not just tidying up; you're writing your success story, one tiny step at a time.

## MAINTAINING MOMENTUM: KEEPING UP THE CLEANING HABIT

Do you know that burst of energy you get when you start a new project? The excitement of Day One is when everything feels possible and you're ready to tackle the world with a mop in one hand and a vacuum in the other. But then comes Day Three, or maybe Week Two, and suddenly, that initial spark fizzles out like a forgotten New Year's resolution. This is where consistency steps in as your best friend. Keeping up with regular cleaning habits is like maintaining a friendship with someone who always has your back. It's not about perfection but about showing up regularly and building a routine through repetition that turns cleaning from a sporadic event into a sustainable part of your life. Maintaining consistency makes you less likely to find yourself knee-deep in chaos. It's about creating a natural and sustainable rhythm, transforming cleaning from an overwhelming chore into a manageable habit.

So, how do you keep that momentum alive? Enter the world of habit stacking. It's a nifty little technique where you piggyback new habits onto existing ones, using the momentum of one to fuel the other. Think of it as adding a soundtrack to your morning routine—you're already brushing your teeth, so why not tidy up the bathroom sink while you're at it? Or maybe you're waiting for your coffee to brew, so take those few minutes to unload the dishwasher. By linking cleaning tasks with routines you already have, you create a seamless flow that makes cleaning feel less like an added burden and more like a natural extension of your day. It's like turning your morning routine into a well-choreographed dance where every step leads to a cleaner home.

Weekly habit reviews are another way to keep your cleaning habits on track. Picture this as a friendly check-in with yourself, a moment to reflect on what's working and what's not. Maybe you've noticed that your Wednesday vacuuming sessions coincide with your favorite TV show, so they keep slipping. Use this time to adjust your schedule, shifting tasks to times that better suit your lifestyle. Weekly habit reviews also allow you to celebrate successes, no matter how small. Did you manage to keep the living room tidy all week? High five! It's about recognizing progress and using it as fuel to keep going.

Let's not overlook the power of visual progress trackers. Imagine a colorful chart on your fridge, each box representing a task completed. These visual cues serve as both a reminder and a motivator, showing you just how much you've accomplished. Seeing those boxes fill up is something profoundly satisfying, like watching a garden grow. It's a tangible representation of your efforts and a visual pat on the back for a job well done. Whether it's a whiteboard, an app, or even a good old-fashioned sticker chart, find a system that speaks to you and lets you see your progress at a glance.

Take Sarah, for example. She once felt like she was constantly cleaning yet never making headway. By implementing habit stacking, she paired her evening wind-down routine with a quick tidy-up, turning it into a nightly ritual. Sarah also set up a visual progress tracker on her kitchen wall, marking each day she completed her cleaning tasks. The simple act of seeing her progress laid out before her was enough to keep her motivated, transforming what felt like a never-ending battle into a series of small victories. Her home became a testament to the power of consistency, proving that maintaining momentum is not only possible but rewarding with a little perseverance and the right tools.

## INVOLVING FAMILY: MAKING IT A TEAM EFFORT

Imagine the symphony of a family cleaning day: everyone contributing their own notes to create a harmonious melody of productivity. Involving your family in cleaning isn't just about dividing up chores. It's about building a team where everyone plays a part, transforming cleaning from solitary drudgery into a collective effort. Shared responsibilities can lighten your load and create a sense of camaraderie. You're not just cleaning; you're strengthening family bonds. It's a great life lesson for kids, too. They learn that maintaining a home is a group effort, not just a parent's task. Plus, working together can reveal hidden talents. You might just discover that your teenager is a whiz with a vacuum or that your spouse has a knack for organizing the pantry like a Tetris champion.

Delegating tasks effectively is key, and creating a family chore chart can work wonders. It's like a game board, where each family member has their own piece to move. Assign age-appropriate tasks that balance challenge with doability. Younger kids can handle dusting low surfaces, while older ones might tackle more intricate tasks like sorting recyclables. Use visual elements like stickers or checkmarks to track completed tasks. This not only makes responsibilities clear but also adds a layer of accountability. And let's not forget the joy of crossing off a task—it's like a mini victory dance on paper. Make sure to rotate responsibilities to keep things fresh, prevent the dreaded "not again" groans, and keep everyone engaged.

But cleaning doesn't have to be all work and no play. Inject a little fun into the mix with cleaning games and challenges. Turn sweeping up into a race, and see who can finish their area first. Or create a treasure hunt where hidden "prizes" are scattered around the house, waiting to be found during cleaning. Family reward systems can be a great motivator, too. Set up a points system where completed tasks earn rewards, like a family movie night or a favorite meal. These incentives transform cleaning from a mere duty into an enjoyable activity, turning even the most reluctant participants into enthusiastic helpers.

Consider the Smith family, who turned their weekly cleaning routine into a family affair. They created a chore chart that assigned tasks based on each family member's strengths and preferences. Saturday mornings transformed into a lively cleaning party, complete with playlists curated by each family member. The kids took turns choosing the music, and they all danced while they dusted and vacuumed. By making cleaning a team effort, the Smiths kept their home tidy and built stronger connections. The kids learned responsibility, and the parents enjoyed the shared sense of achievement. It wasn't just about a clean house but about creating memories and reinforcing family ties.

Involving family in cleaning isn't just about getting the job done faster. It's about teaching teamwork, sharing responsibilities, and having fun. You transform cleaning from a chore into a family tradition by delegating tasks, adding a dose of creativity, and incorporating rewards. So gather the troops, roll up your sleeves, and let the cleaning symphony begin.

## REWARD SYSTEMS: CELEBRATING PROGRESS AND SUCCESS

Remember that feeling of triumph when you finished a big project, and someone gave you a high five or a gold star? Well, guess what? Cleaning can feel like that too. Rewarding yourself for a job well done isn't just for kids; it's a powerhouse strategy for motivating your ADHD brain. By celebrating your progress, you reinforce positive behaviors, making it more likely you'll want to repeat them. Imagine this: you've just spent an hour decluttering your living room and reward yourself with a favorite snack or a quick episode of that show you're obsessed with. Instant gratification can be a powerful motivator, especially for ADHD folks. It gives you that dopamine hit your brain craves, making the act of cleaning feel less like a chore and more like an accomplishment. But don't overlook the long-term rewards, either. These are like the carrot at the end of the stick, motivating you to keep going with the promise of something delightful once you reach your goal. Maybe it's a new book you've been eyeing or a weekend outing you've been dreaming about.

Now, let's get creative with how we reward our cleaning efforts. Have you considered a points-based reward system? Picture it as a game where each task earns you points, and those points can be traded for rewards. Dusting the shelves? That's five points. Tackling the laundry pile? Ten points. Once you've accumulated enough points, you can cash them in for something you enjoy, like a dinner out or a new gadget. If material rewards don't float your boat, consider non-material rewards. A leisurely family outing to the park or a cozy movie night at home can be just as satisfying. The key is to choose rewards that genuinely motivate you, creating a sense of anticipation and excitement.

Personalizing your rewards is crucial. What motivates one person might not work for another, so it's essential to tailor your system to fit your preferences. Some might find joy in a personal reward jar.

Every time you complete a task, you drop a note or a token into the jar, and when it's full, you treat yourself to something special. It's a tangible way to see your progress, and let's be honest, who doesn't love a little jar full of good vibes? Personalizing rewards means you're more likely to stay engaged and motivated, because you've crafted a system that resonates with your unique tastes and desires.

Consider the story of Lily, a reader who struggled to maintain her cleaning routine. She implemented a points-based system, where each completed task earned her a point. Once she reached 50 points, she treated herself to a spa day. The anticipation of a relaxing day off motivated her to keep up with her cleaning tasks, turning a once-dreaded chore into an exciting challenge. Meanwhile, Jake found that non-material rewards worked best for him. After a week of consistent cleaning, he'd reward himself with a relaxing hike or an afternoon spent painting. These activities recharged his creative batteries and provided the motivation he needed to maintain his tidying efforts.

Rewards aren't just about the payoff; they're about creating a positive cycle of reinforcement that keeps you motivated and engaged. By acknowledging your efforts and celebrating your successes, you transform cleaning from a mundane task into an opportunity for growth and satisfaction. Whether it's a small treat or a grand adventure, let your rewards reflect your achievements and inspire you to keep moving forward.

## INTEGRATING CLEANING INTO DAILY ROUTINES

Imagine if cleaning could blend into your day just as seamlessly as your morning coffee or that quick scroll through social media. Integrating cleaning into daily routines isn't about adding more to your plate but weaving it into what you're already doing. Picture this: instead of dedicating a chunk of your weekend to tackle the never-ending pile of laundry, you incorporate mini-tasks into your daily life. This approach reduces the burden of cleaning, making it feel less like a chore and more like a natural part of your day. Think of it as turning cleaning into a background harmony rather than a blaring solo.

One effective strategy is to pair cleaning tasks with existing daily activities. For instance, while you're waiting for your coffee to brew in the morning, use that time to wipe down the kitchen counters or unload the dishwasher. It's about using those pockets of idle time efficiently, turning the mundane moments into opportunities for tidying up. Or consider this: as you brush your teeth before bed, why not use the time to scrub the bathroom sink quickly? Establishing morning and evening routines that incorporate small cleaning tasks can make a world of difference. You get the benefit of a tidier home without feeling like you've sacrificed your downtime.

The beauty of integrating cleaning into daily routines lies in its ability to maintain a consistently tidy environment without the overwhelm of marathon cleaning sessions. When cleaning becomes a regular part of your routine, it feels less daunting and more manageable. It's like brushing your teeth—you do it regularly, so it never becomes a monumental task. This continuous approach prevents clutter from accumulating, and your home remains in a state of order. Plus, when you're not faced with a massive cleaning session at the end of the week, you free up time for activities you genuinely enjoy.

Let's look at some practical examples. Ever find yourself glued to the TV during commercial breaks? Instead of fast-forwarding through them, use those few minutes to tidy up your living room. Fluff the pillows, straighten magazines, or sort through the pile of mail that's been breeding on the coffee table. It's amazing how much you can accomplish in those short bursts, turning what was once idle time into productive cleaning sessions. Or how about incorporating a quick declutter session into your lunch break? Spend five minutes organizing your workspace or clearing out the fridge. It's like hitting a reset button in the middle of your day, leaving you with a sense of accomplishment and a tidier space.

Consider the story of Ella, who used to approach cleaning with dread, always putting it off until her home felt like a disaster zone. She decided to integrate cleaning into her daily routine, pairing tasks with activities she already did. She's dusting the living room shelves while waiting for her tea to steep. During her daughter's nap time, she'd quickly sweep the kitchen floor. These small, consistent efforts transformed her home into a place of order and calm. By the time the weekend rolled around, she found herself with more free time and less stress. Cleaning no longer felt like a burden but an easy, integrated part of her life.

Integrating cleaning into your daily routines is about finding those natural pauses in your day and filling them with productive yet simple tasks. It's about creating a rhythm where cleaning flows effortlessly alongside your other activities, reducing the stress of clutter and leaving you with a consistently tidy home. So, seize the moment next time you're waiting for water to boil or a show to return from break. You might be surprised at how these little pockets of time add up to a cleaner, more organized home.

## TECHNOLOGY AS AN ALLY: LEVERAGING DIGITAL TOOLS

Imagine having a personal assistant who never tires, never forgets, and is always at your beck and call. No, I'm not talking about some mythical creature but about the technology right at your fingertips. In today's world, digital tools can simplify and enhance the cleaning process, streamlining task management to make even the most daunting chore list feel achievable. Think of technology as your trusty sidekick in the battle against chaos. With the right apps and gadgets, you can transform cleaning from a dreaded task into something that fits seamlessly into your life.

Let's start with cleaning reminder apps. These nifty little tools are like having a personal cheerleader who nudges you (gently, of course) to tackle those tasks you've been putting off. Apps like "Tody" or "Remember the Milk" can help you schedule cleaning sessions, send reminders, and even break tasks down into manageable bites. Imagine getting a polite ping when it's time to tackle the bathroom or declutter the living room. These apps help you stay on track, making sure nothing slips through the cracks. Then there's the magic of virtual assistants. Whether it's Alexa, Siri, or Google Assistant, these digital helpers can set timers, create task lists, and even play your favorite cleaning playlist to keep you motivated.

But how do you make the most of these digital wonders? Setting up automated reminders is a game-changer. Picture this: you set a recurring reminder for every Monday to vacuum, and suddenly, it becomes less of a chore and more of a routine. With a few taps, you can have your smartphone or smart speaker gently nudge you when it's time to get cleaning. Use your virtual assistant to set specific cleaning tasks for the week, and watch as the chaos begins to organize itself. It's like having your own personal butler, minus the suit and accent.

Of course, with great power comes great responsibility, and it's easy to fall into the trap of over-relying on technology. It can quickly become overwhelming when your phone buzzes more than a beehive. Limiting app notifications is crucial. Choose only the most important reminders so you're not inundated with constant pings. Technology should be an aid, not a stressor, so make sure it enhances your cleaning routine rather than complicating it. Balance is key; sometimes, a good old-fashioned paper list works wonders alongside digital tools.

Using technology to your advantage can turn cleaning from a dreaded task into an organized, manageable affair. By incorporating apps and virtual assistants, you streamline your cleaning routine, making it efficient and less of a mental burden. Just remember, technology is there to help, not to overwhelm. Find the balance that works for you, and enjoy the satisfaction of a well-maintained home with a little help from your digital allies.

## DIY SOLUTIONS: COST-EFFECTIVE CLEANING HACKS

Have you Ever been staring at a grocery store aisle full of cleaning products, feeling like you've entered a chemist's lab? The endless options, each promising to be more powerful than the last, can leave you dizzy and your wallet lighter. But here's the thing: some of the best cleaning solutions are already hiding in your pantry, waiting for their moment to shine. That's right, we're talking about DIY cleaning hacks that save you money and cut down on unnecessary chemicals. Let's face it, who needs a degree in chemistry to keep a clean home? With a few simple ingredients and a dash of creativity, you can create homemade cleaning solutions that are as effective as they are eco-friendly.

Take vinegar and baking soda, for example. These two humble kitchen staples are like the dynamic duo of cleaning. Need to tackle a clogged drain? Pour half a cup of baking soda down the drain, followed by half a cup of vinegar. Let the fizzing magic happen, wait about 15 minutes, then rinse with hot water. Voilà! A clear drain without the harsh chemicals. Or perhaps your microwave has seen better days after a few too many exploded leftovers. Place a bowl of water with a splash of vinegar inside, microwave it for a few minutes, and let the steam loosen the gunk. A quick wipe later, and your microwave looks brand new. It's like having a cleaning genie at your fingertips, minus the three wishes.

The environmental benefits of these DIY solutions are nothing to sneeze at, either. By swapping out commercial cleaners for home-made alternatives, you're reducing your chemical footprint and doing Mother Earth a favor. Less packaging means less waste, and fewer chemicals mean cleaner waterways. It's a win-win for both your home and the planet. Plus, you get the bonus of knowing exactly what's in your cleaning products, giving you peace of mind and a healthier home environment. And who doesn't love the idea of a cleaner home and a cleaner conscience?

## REAL-LIFE EXAMPLE: DIY SUCCESS STORY

Meet Jessica, a reader who decided to overhaul her cleaning routine after realizing how much she was spending on commercial products. Armed with a few online recipes and a sense of adventure, she whipped up her first batch of all-purpose cleaner using vinegar, water, and a few drops of essential oil for fragrance. Not only did her home smell like a fresh meadow, but she also noticed a significant reduction in her cleaning expenses. Jessica even enlisted her kids in the fun, turning DIY cleaning into a family activity. Her home became a testament to the power of simplicity, proving that sometimes the best solutions are hiding in plain sight.

DIY cleaning solutions aren't just about saving a buck; they're about taking control of your home environment, one homemade cleaner at a time. By embracing these cost-effective hacks, you're lightening your cleaning load and doing your bit for the planet. So next time you reach for that expensive cleaner, remember that your pantry might hold the key to a sparkling home—and a fatter wallet.

## REFLECTING ON PROGRESS: USING JOURNALS AND CHECKLISTS

Imagine, for a moment, that your cleaning efforts are like a grand expedition. It may not involve scaling Everest, but maintaining a tidy home can feel just as daunting. This is where reflection swoops in like a trusty guide, helping you navigate the peaks and valleys of clutter. Reflecting on your progress isn't just about patting yourself on the back; it's about increasing your self-awareness and understanding what works, what doesn't, and why those socks always seem to vanish into your laundry basket's mysterious Bermuda Triangle. By pausing and looking back, you gain invaluable insights into your habits and patterns, allowing you to make informed decisions moving forward. It's the secret ingredient that transforms tidying from a mindless chore into an opportunity for growth and improvement.

Enter the world of journaling, where your thoughts and experiences find their home on paper. Keeping a cleaning journal might sound about as exciting as watching paint dry, but bear with me. This little book of musings becomes a treasure trove of insights, capturing your daily cleaning reflections. Perhaps today you discovered that tackling the bathroom first thing in the morning sets a positive tone for the day. Write it down! Or maybe you learned that vacuuming during your favorite podcast makes the task less of a bore. Note it! Journaling tracks your progress and helps you set and achieve weekly goals. Reviewing your entries allows you to identify patterns and make adjustments, ensuring that your cleaning routine evolves with you. It's like having a personal coach who's always there to cheer you on.

Checklists are another powerful ally in the battle against clutter. These trusty lists break down tasks into bite-sized, manageable chunks, making even the most overwhelming cleaning session feel achievable. A customizable task list is your secret weapon, allowing you to prioritize and adapt tasks to fit your needs. Some days require a laser focus on the kitchen, while others might call for a full-scale assault on the entire house. By creating a checklist reflecting your priorities, you maintain a sense of control and direction. Plus, crossing items off a list is profoundly satisfying—it's like a mini victory dance for your brain, complete with confetti and a marching band.

Take, for example, the story of Michael, a reader who found himself drowning in clutter and chaos. He decided to keep a cleaning journal, jotting down his thoughts and observations each day. As he reviewed his entries, he noticed that cleaning in short bursts was more effective than marathon sessions. Michael also discovered that he felt more accomplished when he tackled tasks immediately after work, rather than putting them off until the weekend. These insights inspired him to create a customizable checklist tailored to his lifestyle. This simple act of reflection transformed his approach to cleaning, leading to a more organized and peaceful home. By tracking his progress, Michael gained a clearer understanding of his habits and cultivated a sense of pride in his achievements.

In the end, reflection, journaling, and checklists are about more than just keeping track of chores. They're tools for self-discovery, helping you unlock the secrets to a more harmonious home. By embracing these practices, you turn cleaning from a mundane task into a meaningful pursuit that fosters growth, awareness, and a touch of humor along the way. So grab that pen, open your journal, and let the adventure begin.

# 6

## PERSONAL GROWTH AND TRANSFORMATION

---

*"The most courageous act is still to think for yourself. Aloud."*

— COCO CHANEL

---

L
et's start with a little confession: I used to think change was as mythical as unicorns. Sure, it sounds magical, but when faced with the reality of changing my cluttered habits, I'd rather chase rainbows than deal with the mountain of mismatched socks piled on my bedroom floor. But here's the thing I discovered—embracing change is like learning to ride a bike. At first, it's all wobbles and scraped knees. But with practice, you find your balance, and suddenly, you're cruising down the street with the wind in your hair. When transforming your living space, understanding the nature of change is key. Accepting new routines and letting go of past habits might seem daunting, but they are the magic spells that turn chaos into calm. It's about reprogramming your brain to see cleaning not as a dreaded task but as an opportunity for personal

growth. Like shedding an old, itchy sweater, you can step into a new way of living that feels fresh and freeing.

Cleaning, believe it or not, can be a catalyst for broader personal transformation. It's not just about tidying up physical spaces; it's also about tidying up your mind. Think of it as a boot camp for self-discipline, where every dish washed and sock paired is a step toward mastering control over your environment. As you get into the cleaning rhythm, you'll find that your ability to manage tasks, make decisions, and even handle unexpected life twists improves. It's like building muscles at the gym—each cleaning session strengthens your resilience and confidence. Suddenly, the world feels less over-whelming, and you have the tools to tackle whatever comes your way. With each box you pack up for donation, you're not just clearing space in your home but making room for new experiences and opportunities.

Navigating change requires strategies that make the transition smoother than a fresh jar of peanut butter. Start with incremental adjustments—small, manageable tweaks that don't send your brain into overdrive. If you've been a night owl, consider shifting your cleaning to a time when your energy levels are higher. Or, if you're used to tackling everything at once, try focusing on one area a day. These tiny shifts can create a ripple effect, leading to more significant transformations over time. Building resilience through change is another crucial aspect. Treat setbacks as stepping stones rather than stumbling blocks. Maybe you didn't get to the laundry today—no biggie. Tomorrow's a new day, and those socks aren't going anywhere. Every attempt, whether successful or not, is progress in disguise. Embrace the journey, and before you know it, you'll be a change ninja, easily slicing through clutter.

Let's sprinkle in some inspiration with stories from people who've experienced transformative changes through cleaning. Take Sarah, for instance. She was once buried under heaps of paper and knick-knacks, each with a story and a reason to stay. But one day, she decided to take control. She started small, clearing her desk drawer, and soon moved on to biggerprojects. With each item she let go, she felt physically and mentally lighter. Her newfound discipline spilled over into other areas of her life, leading to a job promotion and deeper connections with friends. Or consider Mark, who turned his cluttered garage into a creative studio. By letting go of unused tools and forgotten projects, he discovered a passion for painting, transforming not just his space but his entire outlook on life. These stories remind us that change is possible, and it often starts with something as simple as picking up a broom and sweeping away the old to make room for the new.

## REFLECTION EXERCISE: CHANGE AND GROWTH

- **Identify a Habit**: Think of one cleaning habit you'd like to change. Maybe it's procrastination or clutter blindness. Write it down.
- **Plan a Small Shift**: What small step can you take today to move toward change? It could be setting a timer for ten minutes or clearing one surface.
- **Reflect on Progress**: At the end of the week, jot down any changes you've noticed in your mindset or environment. Celebrate even the tiniest victories.

## PERSONAL GROWTH THROUGH CLEANING: FINDING MEANING

Cleaning isn't just about banishing dust bunnies or making sure the laundry pile doesn't become sentient. It's a chance to explore deeper aspects of personal growth and self-discovery. Think of it as a reflective practice, almost like meditation, but with more vacuums involved. As you clean, you might ponder life's big questions: "Why do I have so many unmatched socks?" or "Do I really need those candy wrappers from last Halloween?" In these moments, you begin to reflect on your values—what really matters to you. This reflection can lead to aligning your space with your life goals, creating an environment that truly supports who you are and who you want to be. It's about making room for the things that resonate with your values and letting go of what doesn't. This process, though simple in concept, can lead to profound insights and shifts in how you view your space and yourself.

A tidy space doesn't just look nice; it serves as fertile ground for creativity and ambition. Imagine your mind as a garden. When it's cluttered with random items and forgotten tasks, it's like trying to plant tomatoes in a field of rocks. But clear away the clutter, leaving you with rich soil where ideas can flourish. A clean environment can inspire creativity, offering mental clarity and focus. It's like opening the windows to let fresh air flood in, bringing with it new possibilities and perspectives. If you've ever tried to write a novel, paint a masterpiece, or even brainstorm your next big project, you know how crucial a tidy space can be. It's not about achieving perfection but creating an environment encouraging you to dream bigger and reach higher. The connection between a clean space and achieving your broader life goals becomes clear when you see how much easier it is to focus on what truly matters without the distraction of clutter.

Introspection might sound like something you'd do on a yoga retreat, but it's a fantastic tool to incorporate into your cleaning routine. As you scrub, sweep, or sort, take a moment to pause and reflect. Consider what each item means to you and why it deserves a spot in your life. This practice turns cleaning into a mindful activity, allowing you to engage with your thoughts and feelings in a new way. Instead of mindlessly dusting, you're actively engaging with your environment, making conscious choices about what to keep and what to let go. You might even find that as you declutter, you're also clearing out mental cobwebs, making room for new thoughts and ideas. This mindfulness in cleaning can lead to a greater understanding of yourself and your place in the world, turning a routine task into a journey of self-discovery.

To imbue cleaning with personal significance, consider creating rituals around it. Rituals are like the secret sauce that makes any task feel special, whether it's lighting a candle before you start or playing your favorite music to set the mood. Maybe you start each cleaning session with a moment of gratitude, acknowledging the space you have and the life you're building within it. Or perhaps you end each session with a reward—a cup of tea and a few minutes to admire your handiwork. These rituals turn cleaning from a mundane chore into a meaningful practice, something you look forward to rather than dread. They remind you that cleaning isn't just about tidying up; it's about honoring your space and yourself. Finding meaning in these everyday actions transforms your relationship with cleaning, making it a source of joy and fulfillment.

## FROM CHAOS TO CALM: ACHIEVING A PEACEFUL HOME

Imagine waking up in a space that feels like a breath of fresh air, where each room invites you to relax rather than run away. That's the magic of transforming chaos into calm. When a cluttered space becomes ordered, it's not just about aesthetics—it's an energy shift. With its tendency to multiply like rabbits, clutter can make you feel like you're carrying a constant weight on your shoulders. It's stressful. Anxiety overflows when you're perpetually searching for your keys or stepping over piles of laundry. But the transition to a tidy space can be a game-changer, reducing stress and anxiety by creating an environment that's as soothing as a warm cup of tea on a chilly day. This shift isn't just about the physical act of tidying up; it's about reclaiming mental space, freeing your mind from the constant background hum of chaos.

A peaceful home is more than just a neat one; it's a sanctuary that nurtures your well-being and mental health. In a tidy environment, focus and productivity naturally increase. Without the distraction of clutter, your mind can better concentrate on the task at hand, whether it's reading a book, working on a project, or simply enjoying a moment of silence. The clarity that comes from a well-organized space can lead to improved decision-making and a more positive outlook on life. It's like opening the curtains to let the sunlight in— everything feels brighter and more manageable. A study from Verywell Mind highlights how a clean space can reduce stress and improve mood, suggesting that the act of cleaning itself can lead to feelings of calmness and control.

Consider incorporating colors and textures that soothe your senses to create a calming space. Think soft blues and greens, which are known to promote tranquility, or cozy textures like plush throws and cushy rugs that invite you to sink in and relax. It's not about mimicking a magazine spread but finding elements that make your space feel personal and comforting. Perhaps it's a gallery wall filled with art that speaks to your soul, or a reading nook with a comfy chair and good lighting. The goal is to create a space that feels like a warm hug at the end of a long day, where each element contributes to a sense of peace and balance.

Let's talk about transformation stories, because who doesn't love a good before-and-after? Take my friend, Laura. Her living room once resembled a storage unit, with stacks of books, scattered toys, and a couch that had more crumbs than a bakery. She decided enough was enough. Over a few weeks, she decluttered, donating items she no longer needed and organizing what remained. She added a soft blue rug and hung sheer curtains that let in natural light. The result? Her living room became a serene space where she could unwind and entertain without the embarrassment of chaos. Or consider Tom, who turned his cluttered garage into a sleek home gym. By clearing out the unnecessary and adding a fresh coat of paint, he created a space that motivated him to work out regularly, enhancing both his physical and mental health.

These transformations aren't about achieving perfection. They're about creating a space that reflects your needs and brings you joy. With each item you declutter and each calming element you add, you're not just tidying up your home; you're crafting a sanctuary that supports your well-being. It's a process that invites you to slow down, breathe deeply, and enjoy the newfound peace that comes with a space well cared for.

## BUILDING NEW HABITS: CONSISTENCY IN PRACTICE

Creating new habits can feel like trying to train a cat to fetch—challenging but not impossible. When it comes to maintaining a tidy home, habits are your trusty sidekicks, ready to step in and keep things running smoothly. The key to building these habits lies in understanding habit loops and triggers. A habit loop is a bit like a well-oiled machine: it starts with a trigger, followed by a routine, and concludes with a reward. Take the simple act of hanging up your coat. As you walk through the door, the chill in the air is the trigger. The routine is placing the coat on a hook; the reward is a clutter-free entrance. By setting up these loops, you can transform tasks into automatic behaviors, making the upkeep of your home less of a chore and more of a natural rhythm.

Establishing consistent practices involves strategizing. Daily routines and checkpoints are invaluable tools in this process. Think of them as your GPS guiding you through the day without veering off course. Start small with a daily routine that includes a few key cleaning tasks. Maybe it's wiping down the kitchen counters after dinner or spending five minutes tidying up the living room before bed. These checkpoints act as gentle reminders, holding you accountable and ensuring you stay on track. It's like having a tiny coach in your pocket, cheering you on with every swipe of the cloth.

And don't forget to adjust these routines as needed—flexibility is your friend, not your foe. If you find that something isn't working, tweak it until it fits comfortably into your life.

Overcoming habitual obstacles is a bit like playing a game of Whac-A-Mole—just as you squash one challenge, another pops up. Breaking old habits requires a mix of patience and strategy. Start by identifying the habits that no longer serve you. Maybe it's the habit of leaving dishes in the sink until they form their own ecosystem, or perhaps it's the tendency to toss clothes on the floor instead of hanging them up. Once you've identified these pesky behaviors, replace them with positive alternatives. If you're visual, consider using reminder notes or setting alarms to keep you focused. And remember, it's okay to slip up. Change isn't a straight line; it's a series of loops and curves. Each step you take, no matter how small, is progress. Celebrate the wins, learn from the setbacks, and keep moving forward.

Let's sprinkle in some inspiration with success stories of habit-building triumphs. Meet Lisa, who once lived amid piles of laundry and stacks of papers. She decided to tackle her clutter with a simple habit: every evening, she set a timer for 10 minutes and focused solely on tidying one area. Over time, this tiny habit grew into a consistent practice, and her home transformed from chaotic to calm. Or consider Jake, who struggled with procrastination and cluttered spaces. He implemented a "one-touch" rule, ensuring every item he picked had a designated spot. This seemingly small change made a world of difference, helping him maintain an organized environment without feeling overwhelmed. These stories remind us that habits aren't built overnight but can lead to significant transformations with patience and perseverance.

Building new habits is like planting seeds in a garden. With care and attention, they grow into powerful tools that help maintain a tidy home. By understanding habit loops, establishing consistent practices, and overcoming obstacles, you can cultivate habits that support a cleaner, more organized life. Remember, each small step counts, and with time, these deliberate actions will blossom into a rhythm that feels as natural as breathing.

## CELEBRATING SUCCESS: RECOGNIZING MILESTONES

Let's face it: cleaning can sometimes feel like trying to empty the ocean with a teaspoon. But every now and then, you need to pause, take a step back, and marvel at the seashells you've collected along the way. Recognizing achievements in tidying isn't just about patting yourself on the back—it's a crucial part of keeping the motivation train chugging along. Whether it's finally organizing that junk drawer or decluttering the entire garage, each accomplishment deserves its moment in the spotlight. Celebrating these victories boosts morale and builds self-esteem, reminding you of your capability to conquer chaos. It's like giving yourself a gold star for adulting, and who doesn't love a bit of sparkle in their life? By acknowledging your progress, you reinforce the positive behavior, making it more likely that you'll continue to tidy up with enthusiasm rather than dread.

Setting milestones is your roadmap to success. They're the little flags you plant along your cleaning journey, marking each significant step forward. Start by identifying what you want to achieve, whether it's a weekly goal like maintaining a tidy living room or a monthly target such as decluttering the attic. These milestones act as checkpoints, providing a clear sense of direction and purpose. They help break down the monumental task of keeping a clean home into bite-sized pieces, making it more manageable and less overwhelming. Once you've set your milestones, make a plan to celebrate them. Maybe you host a tidy home gathering, inviting friends over to admire your hard work and enjoy a clutter-free space. It's a chance to share your achievements with others, turning what could be a solitary task into a communal celebration. Or perhaps you prefer personal rewards, like attending a movie night or indulging in your favorite dessert.

The key is to choose something that feels like a genuine reward, a little indulgence that makes the effort worthwhile.

Let's bring in some real-life inspiration with stories from those celebrating their cleaning successes. Take Lily, for instance, who set a goal to keep her kitchen tidy for a month. She tackled a new area every week, from the pantry to the dreaded Tupperware cabinet. At the end of the month, she celebrated by hosting a small dinner party, turning her kitchen into the heart of the home once more. Her friends marveled at the transformation, and the compliments reinforced her commitment to maintaining the space. Then there's Dave, who decided to declutter his wardrobe one weekend. As a reward, he donated the clothes he no longer needed and used the extra room to create a cozy reading nook, complete with a comfy chair and a small bookshelf. This tangible transformation improved his living space and served as a daily reminder of his achievement.

These stories highlight the power of celebration in the cleaning process. They show that recognizing milestones isn't just about ticking boxes—it's about creating moments of joy and reflection amid the daily grind. By celebrating your successes, no matter how small, you infuse the task of cleaning with positivity and purpose. It's a reminder that you're not just tidying up but creating a home that reflects your values and aspirations. So throw that dinner party, indulge in that slice of cake, and relish the satisfaction of a job well done.

## CREATING A VISION FOR YOUR HOME: SETTING GOALS

Imagine waking up in a space that reflects who you are and where you want to go. That's the power of setting a vision for your home. It's not just about tidying up; it's about creating a roadmap that guides your cleaning efforts with clarity and purpose. Think of it as the North Star for your domestic endeavors, a guiding light that keeps you on track when the clutter threatens to take over. When you have a clear vision, each cleaning session becomes a step toward that bigger picture, turning a daunting task into a meaningful pursuit. Whether creating a cozy reading nook or a minimalist kitchen, having a vision ensures you're moving stuff around and toward a space that truly supports your life and aspirations.

Developing a home vision doesn't require a crystal ball—just creativity and practical tools. Start with a vision board, a visual collage of everything you want your home to be. Grab some old magazines, scissors, and glue, and let your imagination run wild. Clip out images, colors, and words that resonate with you and arrange them on a board or in a digital format. This visual representation constantly reminds you of your goals, sparking motivation whenever you glance at it. Writing down your goals can be equally powerful for those who prefer words over pictures. Describe in detail what your ideal home looks like, feels like, and how it functions. Do you want more natural light, a clutter-free kitchen, or a dedicated hobby space? These written goals act as a blueprint, providing direction and keeping you focused on the endgame.

Once you have a vision in place, it's essential to track your progress. Progress journals are an excellent tool for this. They allow you to document your cleaning journey, noting accomplishments and areas needing more attention. Each entry becomes a snapshot of your progress, a record of the steps you've taken toward making your vision a reality. You might jot down your weekly accomplishments, like finally organizing the pantry, or reflect on challenges, such as that stubborn pile of papers on the desk. Over time, these journals become a testament to your hard work and determination, a tangible reminder that even the most minor steps contribute to the larger goal. They also provide an opportunity for reflection, helping you assess what's working and what might need to be adjusted.

Consider the story of Emily, who transformed her cluttered apartment into a serene oasis by setting clear goals and tracking her progress. She began with a vision board with images of airy living rooms and streamlined kitchens. With her vision in mind, she tackled each room one by one, documenting her progress in a journal. She celebrated small victories, like clearing her bedroom of unnecessary furniture, and learned from setbacks, such as when she underestimated the storage needed for her beloved book collection. By staying focused on her vision and using progress journals to track her journey, Emily created a home that reflected her personality and supported her lifestyle. Her transformation serves as a reminder that any space can become a sanctuary with a clear vision and steady progress.

Or take Michael, who turned a cramped, cluttered garage into a functional workshop by setting specific goals and diligently tracking his progress. He envisioned a space where he could pursue his woodworking hobby without tripping over old tools and forgotten projects. With a clear picture of his ideal workshop, he methodically cleared out the clutter, documenting each step in a journal. He set weekly goals, such as installing new shelving or organizing his tool collection, and celebrated each milestone with a sense of accomplishment. His garage, once a chaotic dumping ground, now represents the power of vision and perseverance. Michael's story shows that with determination and a clear plan, even the most challenging spaces can be transformed into something functional and inspiring.

## CONNECTING WITH THE COMMUNITY: SHARING YOUR STORY

In the hustle and bustle of our daily lives, it's easy to feel like you're wrestling with your clutter all alone. But here's the thing: you're not. There's a whole world of folks out there who are in the same boat, paddling through piles of laundry and stacks of paperwork, just like you. Connecting with a community can be like finding an oasis in the desert—a place where you can share your experiences, swap tips, and get a hearty dose of encouragement when you need it most.

Building connections with others who understand the unique challenges of managing a home with ADHD is not only comforting but also empowering. When you share your struggles and victories, you create a ripple effect, allowing others to see they're not alone and that change is possible. It's a bit like forming your own personal cheerleading squad, ready to celebrate your successes and lift you up when things get tough.

So, how do you share your cleaning journey with the world? Social media platforms and community forums are a great starting point. They offer a space where you can post updates, share photos, and engage with others who are on a similar path. Platforms like Instagram and Facebook have thriving communities dedicated to decluttering and home organization, filled with individuals eager to offer support and advice. Don't be afraid to put yourself out there. Whether it's a post about finally tackling that mountain of dishes or a before-and-after shot of your newly organized closet, these platforms allow you to connect with others who will cheer you on every step of the way. Community forums like those on Reddit platforms can also be invaluable. They offer a more intimate setting where you can ask questions, share tips, and receive feedback from those who genuinely understand the challenges of keeping a tidy home while juggling the complexities of ADHD.

Engaging with others who share similar experiences can profoundly impact your cleaning journey. The benefits of community involvement extend far beyond the immediate satisfaction of a well-organized home. By engaging with others, you gain access to a wealth of shared tips and advice that can make a world of difference in your approach to cleaning. From discovering new organizational hacks to learning about the latest cleaning tools, the collective knowledge of a community is a treasure trove of information. More importantly, these connections offer emotional support. When you're feeling overwhelmed or discouraged, knowing a group of people has your back can provide the motivation you need to keep going. It's about creating a network of support, a safety net that catches you when you stumble and propels you forward when you succeed.

Let's take a look at some community success stories, shall we? Take Jenna, for instance. She joined an online decluttering group after feeling stuck in a cycle of clutter and chaos. Through the group, she found practical tips and a sense of belonging. She shared her progress regularly, receiving encouragement and feedback that kept her motivated. As she decluttered her home, she realized she was also decluttering her mind, making room for new opportunities and experiences. Or consider Alex, who turned to a local ADHD support group for advice on managing his home. The group introduced him to the concept of a "body double"—having someone present while he cleaned, which helped him stay focused and accountable. The support and camaraderie he found in the group transformed his approach to cleaning, turning it from a dreaded chore into a manageable task. These stories remind us that community is more than just a group of people; it's a source of strength, inspiration, and transformation.

## SUSTAINING CHANGE: LONG-TERM STRATEGIES FOR SUCCESS

Keeping your home tidy over the long haul might feel like trying to keep a puppy in a bubble bath—chaotic at best and downright impossible at worst. One of the biggest hurdles is the tendency to slip back into old habits. You know the ones: leaving dishes in the sink for "later" (which somehow turns into next week) or letting mail accumulate until it resembles the Leaning Tower of Pisa. It's like your brain gravitates towards clutter, beckoning you back to familiar patterns. The struggle is real, but fear not! With some savvy strategies, you can outsmart those sneaky old habits and maintain a tidy haven.

The first step is to embrace regular reassessments—your secret weapon against clutter creep. Think of it as a quick check-in with your space to see what's working and what needs a little tweak. Every few months, take a walk through your home with a fresh set of eyes. Are those storage solutions still doing their job, or is it time for a little reorganization? Regularly assessing your space can nip problems in the bud before they spiral out of control. This practice helps prevent clutter from creeping back in and keeps your home functioning like a well-oiled machine.

Periodic decluttering sessions are another crucial element in the fight against chaos. Set aside time every season to go through your belongings discerningly. Ask yourself if each item still serves a purpose or if it's just taking up precious real estate. You might find that those jeans you've been holding onto since high school no longer fit your style—or your waistline. Letting go of things that no longer serve you is liberating and creates space for what truly matters. And remember, decluttering doesn't have to be a solo mission. Enlist a friend or family member to help, turning it into a fun and productive event.

Flexibility is your best friend when it comes to sustaining change, especially when life throws curveballs your way. Maybe you've moved to a new home, added a family member, or started working from home. These changes require a shift in how you manage your space. Adaptability means being open to changing your systems and routines to fit your current circumstances. Perhaps that storage solution that worked wonders in your old apartment is less effective in your new house. Be willing to adjust and experiment until you find what works for you. It's all about evolving and finding creative solutions that suit your lifestyle.

Let's look at some success stories of folks who've managed to keep their homes tidy over the long term. Take Lisa, for example. She once struggled with a cluttered kitchen that seemed to attract gadgets like bees to honey. After a significant decluttering session, she committed to a "one in, one out" rule, ensuring that an old one had to go for every new item she brought in. This simple strategy helped her maintain a clutter-free kitchen for years. Or consider Tom, who used to have a closet bursting at the seams. He implemented a seasonal wardrobe rotation, storing off-season clothes in labeled bins and only keeping current items in his closet. This approach kept his closet organized, making getting dressed in the morning a breeze.

These stories highlight that sustaining change is an ongoing process that requires vigilance, creativity, and a willingness to adapt. By regularly reassessing your space, embracing periodic decluttering, and remaining flexible to life's changes, you can create a home that stays tidy and welcoming over time. Remember, it's not about achieving perfection but creating a space that supports and enhances your life.

As we wrap up this chapter, remember that maintaining a tidy home involves adapting and evolving strategies over time. Your home is a reflection of your life, and as life changes, so should your approach to maintaining order. Embrace flexibility and creativity, and stay committed to the routines and strategies that work for you. Whether it's periodic decluttering, regular reassessments, or simply adjusting to life's changes, keep your focus on long-term success. Your tidy home is within reach, and the journey is as important as the destination. Now, let's move forward with a renewed sense of purpose and commitment to maintaining the space that brings you joy and peace.

# YOU'VE REACHED THE END—NOW, LET'S HELP SOMEONE ELSE!

***Your Words Have Power!***

> *"Small acts, when multiplied by millions of people, can change the world."*

— HOWARD ZINN

You made it! 🎉 Tidy-ish wasn't just about cleaning—it was about finding a way to make your home work for YOU. If this book has helped you—whether by making tidying less overwhelming, giving you fresh ideas, or just making you feel less alone—imagine how much it could help someone else!

**Would you take a moment to share your thoughts?**

Most people choose books based on reviews. Your words could be the boost that helps someone stop feeling stuck and start making progress. It takes just a minute, but your review could help...

✨ One more person let go of cleaning shame.

✨ One more ADHD brain find a system that actually works.

✨ One more home feel like a peaceful place to be.

If Tidy-ish made a difference for you, I'd love to hear about it! Leaving a review is the easiest way to help more people find the support they need.

From the bottom of my heart—thank you for being part of this journey. Your support, your story, and your progress mean everything! 🤍

**Alex Rivers x**

# CONCLUSION

Well, my friend, we've come to the end of our tidy-ish journey together. Can you believe it? We've navigated through the chaos of clutter, the perils of procrastination, and the challenges of maintaining a manageable home with an ADHD brain. It's been quite the adventure, hasn't it?

Throughout this book, we've explored strategies tailored specifically for individuals with ADHD, recognizing that our unique minds require equally unique approaches. We've learned that it's not about achieving picture-perfect spaces but about creating homes that work with our natural tendencies and support our well-being.

Let's take a quick stroll down memory lane, shall we? In the first chapter, we laid the foundation for change by understanding our ADHD brains and embracing self-compassion. We discovered the power of starting small and celebrating progress, no matter how incremental. Chapter two introduced us to game-changing techniques like time-blocking and task chunking, helping us break down the overwhelming into manageable ones. In the third chapter, we explored ADHD-friendly cleaning systems, from visual cues to sensory-friendly tools, transforming cleaning from a dreaded chore into an engaging activity.

Chapter four delved into the emotional aspects of cleaning, guiding us through decluttering sentimental items and overcoming negative past experiences. We learned to build resilience and find motivation through rewards and joyful cleaning practices. The fifth chapter focused on practical implementation, integrating cleaning into our daily lives through habit stacking, technology, and family involvement. Finally, in chapter six, we discovered the transformative power of cleaning for our homes and our personal growth and well-being.

So, what are the key takeaways from this tidy-ish adventure? First and foremost, remember that progress, not perfection, is the goal. Embrace the concept of "good enough" and celebrate every small victory along the way. Secondly, find the best strategies for your unique brain and lifestyle. Whether it's visual cues, time-blocking, or dancing while you declutter, lean into what brings you joy and success. Finally, recognize that a tidy home is not just about the physical space but about the mental and emotional benefits it provides. A manageable home can be a catalyst for reduced stress, increased productivity, and a greater sense of control over your life.

Now, my friend, it's time to take these insights and run with them. Don't wait for the perfect moment to start—the perfect moment is now. Choose one small change you can make today, whether it's setting a timer for a five-minute tidy session or decluttering a single drawer. Remember, every journey begins with a single step, and every small action contributes to the larger goal of a more manageable home.

As you embark on this tidy-ish path, know you are not alone. Countless others, myself included, have faced the same challenges and triumphed. Embrace the power of community, sharing your experiences and learning from the stories of others. You never know who you might inspire, what valuable insights you might gain, or who you might meet. And remember, setbacks are a normal part of the process. When you stumble, simply dust yourself off (figuratively and literally) and keep moving forward. Progress is a journey, not a destination.

Before we part ways, I am grateful for your commitment to this journey. As someone who has navigated the ups and downs of maintaining a home with ADHD, I know firsthand the courage and determination it takes. Your efforts, no matter how small they may seem, are a testament to your strength and resilience. Be proud of every step you take towards a more manageable home and a more fulfilling life.

As you continue on this path, remember that the skills and habits you develop through tidying extend far beyond the physical space. The self-awareness, resilience, and adaptability you cultivate will serve you in countless areas of your life. Embrace the growth and transformation that comes with each small victory, knowing that a tidy home is just the beginning of a more harmonious and joyful existence.

So, my tidy-ish friend, go forth and conquer the clutter. Embrace the journey, celebrate the progress, and know that a more manageable home is within your reach. The future is bright, and I have no doubt that you will continue to amaze yourself with what you can achieve. Here's to a tidy-ish home, a tidy-ish mind, and a tidy-ish life. You've got this! x

# RESOURCES & FURTHER READING – BOOKS, APPS, AND ADHD-FRIENDLY TOOLS

- American Society for the Positive Care of Children. (n.d.). *Unlocking success: Reward systems for children with ADHD*. Retrieved from https://americanspcc.org/unlocking-success-reward-systems-for-children-with-adhd/
- Apartment Therapy. (n.d.). *5 ways to tweak your cleaning routine if you have ADHD*. Retrieved from https://www.apartmenttherapy.com/adhd-cleaning-routine-tips-36991822
- CHADD. (n.d.). *Improving the lives of people affected by ADHD*. Retrieved from https://chadd.org/
- Clutter Free Now. (n.d.). *How to declutter your home with mindfulness*. Retrieved from https://clutterfreenow.com/how-to-declutter-your-home-with-mindfulness/
- Day Optimizer. (n.d.). *Mastering time blocking for ADHD: Your ultimate guide to better focus*. Retrieved from https://dayoptimizer.com/adhd/mastering-time-blocking-for-adhd-your-ultimate-guide-to-better-focus/
- Deepwrk. (n.d.). *ADHD cleaning checklist and 14 tips to transform chaos*. Retrieved from https://www.deepwrk.io/blog/adhd-cleaning-checklist
- DSO Ontario. (n.d.). *Creating a sensory-friendly home - Tip sheet*. Retrieved from https://www.dsontario.ca/housing-toolkit/creating-a-sensory-friendly-home-tip-sheet
- Focus Bear. (n.d.). *ADHD cleaning checklist: Simplifying the process for a tidier home*. Retrieved from https://www.focusbear.io/blog-post/adhd-cleaning-checklist-simplifying-the-process-for-a-tidier-home
- Leantime. (n.d.). *ADHD tools for adults: Task management strategies & success*. Retrieved from https://leantime.io/mastering-task-management-for-adhd
- Millennial Therapy. (n.d.). *Habit-forming 101, Part 1: How to build habits with ADHD*. Retrieved from https://www.millennialtherapy.com/anxiety-therapy-blog/how-to-build-habits-with-adhd
- MW Psychology. (n.d.). *ADHD case studies, Roswell, GA*. Retrieved from https://www.mwpsychology.com/casestudies/adhd
- Neurodiverging. (n.d.). *An ADHD-friendly way to make a cleaning routine that works for you*. Retrieved from https://www.neurodiverging.com/an-adhd-friendly-way-to-make-a-cleaning-routine-that-works-for-you/

- Real Simple. (n.d.). *10 expert-backed cleaning strategies if you struggle with ADHD*. Retrieved from https://www.realsimple.com/cleaning-strategies-for-adhd-7724706
- Rula. (n.d.). *How ADHD and hoarding are linked*. Retrieved from https://www.rula.com/blog/hoarding-adhd
- Tiimo. (n.d.). *ADHD and organization: Proven strategies to simplify your life*. Retrieved from https://www.tiimoapp.com/resource-hub/adhd-at-work-how-to-get-organized
- Verywell Mind. (n.d.). *Benefits of habit stacking for ADHD*. Retrieved from https://www.verywellmind.com/habit-stacking-definition-steps-benefits-for-adhd-6751145
- Verywell Mind. (n.d.). *The connection between cleanliness and mental health*. Retrieved from https://www.verywellmind.com/how-mental-health-and-cleaning-are-connected-5097496
- Verywell Mind. (n.d.). *The neurodivergent guide to cleaning up*. Retrieved from https://www.verywellmind.com/the-neurodivergent-guide-to-cleaning-up-7372087
- Wellness Speaks. (n.d.). *Creating a nontoxic haven: The importance of safe household products for autism and ADHD*. Retrieved from https://www.wellness-speaks.com/blogs/creating-a-nontoxic-haven-the-importance-of-safe-household-products-for-autism-and-adhd

Made in the USA
Coppell, TX
22 December 2025